BRYAN CAPLAN

Self Help is Like a Vaccine

Essays on Living Better

First edition

Edited by Brian Mandeville and Aditya Ohri

To Tyler Cowen, the big brother who has been helping me help myself for over thirty years

Contents

III   Professor Homeschool

IV   How to Dale Carnegie

Part I

Unilateral Action

Self-Help Is Like a Vaccine

EI's Andrew Biggs has a totally reasonable piece arguing that Americans' unhealthy lifestyles are a major cause of America's high Covid mortality rate:

Americans entered the Covid pandemic in much poorer health than citizens of other developed countries. For instance, over 27,000 U.S Covid deaths list diabetes as a comorbidity, accounting for 16% of total Covid-related fatalities. But what if instead of having the highest diabetes rate among rich countries the U.S. had the same rate as Australia, with less than half the U.S. level? The same holds for obesity, listed as a comorbidity in 4% of Covid cases. Forty percent of Americans are obese, the highest in the developed world and over twice the OECD average. U.S. death rates from heart disease are also higher than most European and Asian countries. Hypertension is listed as a comorbidity in 22% of Covid deaths. If Americans simply had the same health status as other high-income countries, it is likely that tens of thousands of lives could have been saved.[1]

The obvious upshot is: *Individuals can and should reduce their risk by switching to healthier lifestyles*. Yet Biggs strangely declares the opposite:

> General practitioners tell me that their Type 2 diabetes patients can tell you their weight and know how it relates to their illness. They know that by losing weight their can reduce their risk of blindness, limb amputations or death. They simply aren't able to do it.

If anything is obvious, however, it is that they simply *are* able to do it. Anyone can. Eat fewer and smaller meals… and you will lose weight. Exercise more… and you will lose weight. Everyone knows this. And everyone can apply their knowledge. Put less food in your mouth, move your body more, and your risk of dying of Covid will crash.

Why then do so many people remain unhealthy, even the midst of an historic pandemic? Because they prefer the pleasure of food and idleness plus the attendant health loss to the pain of hunger and exertion plus the attendant health gain. To quote Al Pacino in *Scent of a Woman*:

> I always knew what the right path was. Without exception, I knew. But I never took it. You know why? It was too damn hard.[2]

If this is all undeniable, why do so many smart people refuse to assent? Social Desirability Bias, naturally.[3] When the truth sounds bad, people say — and perhaps even believe — the patently untrue. As I've explained before:[4]

> "Sorry, I can't come to your party." This common excuse is almost always literally false.[5] You're working? Unless your boss chains you to your desk, you can come to the party. You're in Paris, and the party's in DC tomorrow? If you can beg, borrow, or steal airfare, you can come to the party. The same goes for most social uses of the word "can't" — everything from "We can't be together" to "I can't help myself."
>
> Why say, "I can't" when the truth is "It's too costly for me" or "I don't feel like it"? Because "I can't" sounds better. It insinuates, "The only reason I'm not doing X is because I lack the ability to do X. Otherwise I would totally do it." "It's too costly for me" and "I don't feel like it" are insulting by comparison. Both blurt, "X simply isn't my top priority. Get used to it." In short, the way we use the word "can't" is a clearcut case of Social Desirability Bias: our all-too-human propensity to lie when the truth sounds bad.[6]
>
> The literally-false "can't" is hardly alone. Social Desirability Bias permeates our diction — i.e., the specific words we choose to use.[7]

What's so awful about sugarcoating the harsh reality that the obese are fully capable of reaching a healthy body weight?

Simple: Sugarcoating *distracts and confuses*. Self-help is

a virtually foolproof solution for obesity; as long as you strict-ly follow the recipe, you won't be obese for long. Ignoring or denying the possibility of self-help discourages people from fixing — or even saving! — their own lives.

One could scoff, "Human beings are weak. What's the point of telling them to diet and exercise for the rest of their lives when we know they won't? We might as well just spare their feelings."

Perhaps, perhaps.

Consider, though, this parallel argument: "Anti-vaxxers are crazy.[7] What's the point of telling them to get vaccinated when we know they won't? We might as well just spare their feelings."

Can you think of any decent objections? Because I definitely can.

1. *There's a continuum of crazy.* Some anti-vaxxers are beyond hope. Others will only bend the knee in the face of overwhelming shame. A great many, however, are only skin deep crazy. Moderate shame — or persistent persuasion — will eventually get the vaccines in their bloodstreams.

2. *Crazy is contagious.* If no one challenges anti-vaxxers, un-decided bystanders are more likely to adopt their crazy ideas. These "converts," in turn, can easily go on to corrupt others. Given how conformist human beings are, the anti-vax move-ment can spread even in the absence of deliberate recruitment efforts. Initially non-crazy people notice the rising prevalence of crazy ideas — and casually become crazy themselves.

3. *Someone's gonna get blamed.* If you refuse to blame anti-vaxxers for their own bad choices, people are likely to look around for someone *else* to blame. For example: "People

would probably be happy to take vaccines, if doctors weren't so arrogant." The result: Instead of "sparing people's feelings" in the aggregate, you wind up *redistributing* the hurt feelings over to innocent bystanders.

What then is the right message to send? This: "Anti-vaxxers are totally able to get vaccinated. The are making bad choices. They should make better choices."

This isn't merely helpful; it is true.

The same goes for obesity. The right message is not: "They are simply unable to lose weight." The right message is: "The obese are totally able to be thin. They are making bad choices. They should make better choices."

This isn't merely helpful; it is true.

The same principle holds for self-help generally. *Self-help is like a vaccine*: When used, it works wonders. The fact that many people refuse to do what works is a flimsy reason to humor them. And it is a terrible reason to endorse clear-cut errors like, "They just can't do it." Anyone can get vaccinated; just roll up your sleeve and let the doctor stick you with the needle. Anyone can be thin; just eat moderately and exercise regularly. And anyone can improve his own life; just stop making excuses and follow the path of prudence.

September 30, 2020

Notes

1. Biggs, Andrew. "Americans' Poor Health Paved the Way for COVID-19 Deaths." *American Enterprise Institute*, September 4, 2020.

2. "Scent of a Woman (1992)." *American Rhetoric: Movie Speech.*
3. Caplan, Bryan. "Social Desirability Bias: How Psych Can Salvage Econo-Cynicism." *EconLog*, April 21, 2014.
4. Caplan, Bryan. "The Diction of Social Desirability Bias." *EconLog*, April 22, 2016.
5. Cowen, Tyler. "Simple Points About Central Banking and Monetary Policy." *Marginal Revolution*, February 19, 2016.
6. Caplan, Bryan. "The Public Goods Model vs. Social Desirability Bias: A Case of Observational Equivalence." *EconLog*, September 4, 2012. Caplan, Bryan. "Demagoguery Explained." *EconLog*, May 3, 2014. "Diction." *Literary Devices.*
7. Weatherspoon, Deborah. "Understanding Opposition to Vaccines." *Healthline*, September 15, 2017.

Say "Can't" With Care

Suppose a student fails a math test. Casual observers will often announce, "He can't do the math."

Or suppose a country has a horrible corruption problem. Casual observers will often announce, "The government can't solve this corruption problem."

In each case, I detect a casual logical fallacy.

Namely: If person X actually does Y, we can legitimately infer, "X *can* do Y." But if person X does not do Y, we cannot legitimately infer that they *can't*. Maybe they don't do Y because they *can't* do Y. Maybe they don't do Y because they *choose not* to do Y.

What's the real story? Figuring that out requires further investigation. Before you declare that, "X can't do Y," start with this simple checklist:

Step 1: See if the actor in question even *tried* to do Y.

Step 2: If the actor tried, examine *how hard* he tried.

Step 3: Look at how successful comparably-able actors are when they try their *very hardest*.

Thus, before you say that a kid who fails a math test "can't" do it, you should examine (a) whether he even tried to pass, (b) if so, how hard he tried, and (c) the pass rate for comparable students who try their very hardest.

Similarly, before you say that a country "can't" solve its corruption problem, you should examine (a) whether the country even tried to do so, (b) if so, how hard it tried, and (c) the success rate for comparable countries that try their very hardest.

You could respond, "Running such an investigation sounds awfully difficult. How do we know whether someone tried? How hard they tried? How do we find comparable actors? How do we know whether the comparable actors 'tried their very hardest?'"

I fully agree. Knowing what someone *can't* do tends to be hard. Which is precisely why you should make such claims with care.

The most egregious misuses of "can't," however, come when even token efforts *reliably* produce success. When someone says, "He can't stop drinking," or "He can't stop cheating," common sense revolts. Maybe you aren't smart enough to pass a math test. But what skill does it take not to consume a beverage? To abstain from sex? Just don't do it — and it is done.

January 15, 2020

10

My Life of Appeasement

Morally speaking, I think taxation is theft. The government has a lot of bad excuses for taking my money without my consent, but no really good reasons.[1] Still, every year, I pay my taxes.

Why don't I stand up for my rights? The obvious reason: If I stood up for my rights by refusing to pay and attacking anyone who tried to make me, I would end up dead or in jail. That's the way the government deals with tax resistors.[2]

Given this bleak forecast, I never openly defy the government. Instead, I practice the opposite strategy: *appeasement*. I find out what the government demands, I comply, and I resume living my rich, fulfilling life. Yes, my rights have been violated. But I'd rather live on my knees than die on my feet. Indeed, I would consider dying on my feet to be not only foolish, but wicked. Life is a gift, even if the government insists on tarnishing it.

Didn't the Munich Agreement prove for all time that appeasement doesn't work?[3] Hardly. Despite its well-hyped failures, appeasement is an incredibly effective social strategy for dealing with the unreasonable and the unjust... also known as 90% of mankind. Whenever someone makes bizarre demands upon me, my default is not to argue. Instead, I weigh the cost of compliance. If that cost is small — and it usually is — I let the babies have their way. If you bump into me in the grocery store, I say "Sorry."

Doesn't that open the floodgates to additional demands? Not in my experience. One symbolic gesture is enough to placate most of the unpleasant characters I encounter. After my concession, we usually go our separate ways. And even when I repeatedly interact with the same unreasonable, unjust person, at least my appeasement makes it hard for them to imagine that they have to get back at me for *my* past wrongs.

Despite their scorn, almost everyone knows that appeasement works. How do I know this? Because everyone appeases to cope with social realities. Recall your day. Did you experience some unreasonable, unjust treatment? Probably. If so, did you escalate the conflict until reason and justice prevailed? Probably not. Why not? Because it would be a Pyrrhic victory, likely to leave you unemployed and alone.

Once people retract the absurd claim that "appeasement doesn't work," they finally unveil their real objection: They have too much pride to appease. "Why should I apologize when she's the one who stepped on my foot?" When people express such attitudes, I usually just appease them and get on with my life. But what I'm silently thinking is: "If you're truly awesome, you shouldn't care what unreasonable, unjust people think."

Does this mean that you should never stand up for what is right? Of course not. But you should pick your battles very carefully. While fighting is far more impulsively satisfying than submitting, you should restrain your impulses in favor of calm reflection. You might be in the wrong. You might be making a mountain out of a molehill. And even if right and proportion are on your side, the real world is not an action movie. You could easily fail — and you have a lot to lose.

August 5, 2014

Notes

1. Huemer, Michael. *The Problem of Political Authority,* 2012.
2. "List of Historical Acts of Tax Resistance." *Wikipedia.*
3. "Munich Agreement." *Wikipedia.*

When to Be Meek

I f you're not getting what you want out of life, people usually advise you to speak up and demand what's coming to you. You'll never get anywhere just saying "please" and "thank you." You've got to stand up and assert yourself.

Strangely, though, most of the people who offer this advice aren't getting what they want out of life, either. If they've really got a foolproof strategy to get ahead, why don't they practice what they preach?

The answer, naturally, is that "demanding what's coming to you" sounds a lot better in theory than it actually works. Standing up for yourself is a high-risk strategy. Yes, it occasionally pays off, but it's far from a sure thing. Sometimes you get nothing but aggravation. And sometimes the whole approach backfires. How? Being demanding causes other people to dislike you. And when people dislike you, they treat you worse.

This doesn't mean that the meek will inherit the earth. But it does mean that meekness is underrated. Although you won't rise to the top of the heap by being meek, you probably won't get hurled to the bottom, either.

"Stand up for yourself" isn't just overrated; it's also misdirected. We're quickest to dispense this advice to the people least likely to benefit from it. Consider: If you have wealth and power, standing up for yourself tends to work well. But we usually advise the wealthy and powerful to be gentle and generous. Perhaps we're just advising them to use their status ethically. But we often couch such advice in prudential terms: "A smart CEO knows that a happy worker is a productive worker." If, on the other hand, you're poor and powerless, standing up for yourself is normally disastrous. If you have little to offer, you have to rely on the goodwill of others. And one of the surest ways to make a bonfire of your accumulated goodwill is to embrace a bad attitude.

Charles Murray's *Coming Apart* doesn't directly discuss the value of meekness.[1] But my analysis is very consistent with Murray's. My speculation:

A major difference between the professional and working classes is that professionals appreciate the wages of meekness. They realize that if you want to move from high school to college, from college to an entry-level job, from an entry-level job to a promotion, you must get in the habit of saying, "Thank you, sir. May I have another?" Even if you're elite in absolute terms, you ascend the hierarchy by showing deference to people who are even more elite than you are. The working class, in contrast, is dysfunctionally assertive. Maybe they put pride and machismo above success; maybe they falsely believe that pride and machismo are a shortcut to success. In either case, as Murray emphasizes, one of the best ways for elites to help is to preach the meekness they've so often and so fruitfully practiced.

Consider this one such sermon.

February 20, 2012

Notes

1. Caplan, Bryan. "An Optimist's Take on Charles Murray's *Coming Apart." EconLog,* January 17, 2012.

Machismo vs. Appeasement

I suspect that the ultimate objection to pacifism and appeasement is that they are *unmanly*.[1] A "real man," brimming over with machismo, stands up for himself no matter what the consequences: Never retreat, never surrender.

The emotional appeal is undeniable. Who can forget this scene from *The Return of the King*?

> Gamling: Too few have come. We cannot
> defeat the armies of Mordor.
> Theoden: No. We cannot. But we will meet
> them in battle nonetheless.[2]

Intellectually, though, the glorification of machismo has no appeal at all. Who are the most macho of men? Criminals. Thugs. Conquerors. I've never heard anyone question the masculinity of Genghis Khan, but he was one of the worst men who ever lived.

Manly values have their uses every now and then. Let us never forget the deeds of Claus von Stauffenberg.[3] But only

17

when the manly values of courage and determination are subordinate to the nerdy values of objectivity and justice.[4]

August 8, 2014

Notes

1. Caplan, Bryan. "The Common-Sense Case for Pacifism." *EconLog*, April 5, 2010. Caplan, Bryan. "My Life of Appeasement." *EconLog*, August 5, 2014.
2. "We cannot defeat the Armies of Mordor." *YouTube*, Dagana, September 6, 2012.
3. Caplan, Bryan. "Tyrannicide: Now in a Theater Near You." *EconLog*, December 31, 2008. "Claus von Stauffenberg." *Wikipedia*.
4. Caplan, Bryan. "Redistributing: Blocking the Revenge of the Nerds?" *EconLog*, June 21, 2007.

The Cause of What I Feel
Is What I Do:
How I Eliminate Pain

O ver the last twenty years, I have experienced a litany of chronic pain: back pain, neck pain, foot pain, knee pain, forearm pain, and tailbone pain. I also experienced bizarre chronic tingling on my scalp. The good news is that I have managed to virtually eliminate every one of these problems.

Perhaps these ills would have gone away on their own, but all my experience says the opposite: Without conscious action, each of these problems would have lingered, compounded, and probably intensified. Fortunately, I have developed a system that works wonders for me. Hopefully it will work for you to, if you ever share my plight.

So how have I overcome my litany of pain problems? Let me start with what *never* works for me.

1. *Doctors*. I have talked to a wide variety of M.D.s about a wide variety of my problems. They have been beyond useless. Most offer nothing better than a *name* for my symptoms. ("Mr. Caplan, you have plantar fasciitis."[1] "Latin, how help-

ful.") Some have given me prescription pills that are chemically equivalent to two non-prescription pills. Some have given me injections that numb the affected area, then leave me no better off than before. Often, they lecture me about unrelated issues just to fill the time. When people ask me if I've "considered surgery," I am astounded by their naivete. If Robin Hanson hadn't made me a medical skeptic, my first-hand experience would have.[2]

2. *Exercise.* Every time I've tried exercising a painful part of my body, I felt my problem getting worse. Lifting stuff made my forearm pain worse. Leaning over made my back pain worse. Running made my foot pain worse. The slogan says, "No pain, no gain." For me, however, the right slogan is: "Pain begets pain." Enduring physical pain simply leads to even more pain in the future.

Then what does work?

1. *Obsessively examine behavior.* Without exception, I've discovered that the cause of my pain is behavioral. In slogan form: *The cause of what I feel is what I do.* Sadly, the details of what causes what are far from obvious; otherwise, all my pain would be extremely short-lived. The best fundamental pain remedy, therefore, is to obsessively search for any behavior that plausibly aggravates your pain. Then test your ideas by mindfully ceasing suspicious activity.

For example, when I had horrible tailbone pain, I naturally suspected that I was sitting the wrong way. So I tried chairs with a wide variety of back angles, until I discovered that a straight 90-degree angle was least painful for me.

Similarly, when my right forearm started hurting a year ago, I eventually noticed that shaking hands horribly aggravated my pain. So I stopped shaking until the pain was a distant memory.

2. *Orthotics, orthotics, orthotics.* Doctors provide expensive verbiage. Your local pharmacy, in contrast, provides cheap salvation. After multiple doctors failed to alleviate my foot pain, I went to the pharmacy and bought every foot product they sold. Some turned out to be useless, but I quickly learned that a simple arch support provided marked pain reduction. This in turn led me to hunt for an even wider variety of arch supports. Ultimately I wound up crazy-gluing a women's arch support on top of a men's arch support — and my foot pain faded into nothingness. As far as I know, I am the world's leading assembler of artisanal foot orthotics.

Another example: When I had tailbone pain, I naturally tried softer chairs. That helped slightly, but I soon resolved to buy and test a dozen different cushions. That, combined with a 90-degree chair, ultimately eliminated my tailbone pain.

3. *Obsessively experiment.* If you're out of *good* behavioral ideas, try *any* idea that crosses your mind. You can usually tell in a minute or two if you're aggravating your problem. When my back was in agony last September, I tried every sleeping posture, bed type, and pillow arrangement I could imagine. I expected almost every idea to fail, but kept trying. Finally I discovered that my back pain upon waking was minimal if I stacked two soft thick pillows horizontally under my abdomen, then placed a flat pillow vertically under my upper chest. After hitting on this inverted t-formation, I further experimented with a wide variety of pillows to enhance the pain-reducing effect.

4. *Focus on proximate causes.* Logically speaking, your "pain-inducing behavioral problem" could be a vitamin deficiency. In practice, however, reasoning from proximate causes is highly reliable. Like causes like: The cause of foot pain is walking or standing the wrong way. The cause of tailbone pain is sitting the wrong way. The cause of forearm pain is grabbing and lifting the wrong way. My last episode of back pain was hard to diagnose, because I was initially in so much pain that *all* behaviors hurt. Once I made progress, however, I was able to discover that my back pain only amplified when I was sitting. This in turn led me to focus on different chairs, back cushions, and the like. Now I'm practically cured.

While this is only one man's experience, my principles have repeatedly worked out of sample for me.[3] When a new form of pain descends upon me, I open up my well-tested toolkit and get to work. Obviously my approach will not work for everyone, but I suspect it will work wonders for 80% of people who mindfully apply it. And even if chronic pain has never troubled you, one day it will. So take heed.

P.S. I got an MRI for my head tingling. As usual, the doctor found nothing and knew no way to help me. Fortunately, I eventually noticed that my head tingled much more whenever I was near a heat vent. So I drastically cut my use of artificial heat, dressed more warmly, and my tingling almost vanished.

March 19, 2020

Notes

1. "Plantar fasciitis." *Mayo Clinic.*
2. Hanson, Robin. "Cut Medicine in Half." *Cato Unbound,* September 10, 2007.
3. "In Sample vs. Out Of Sample." *YouTube*, Udacity, June 6, 2016

Omniscience is Not Enough

I 've repeatedly debated with Tyler Cowen about the epistemic value of betting.[1] Long before I amassed my 21-bet winning streak, I've argued that betting about substantive intellectual questions does all of the following:[2]

1. Greatly improves the quality of our thinking by converting vague, ambiguous language into clear, specific claims.

2. Greatly improves the quality of discourse by incentivizing the rationally ignorant and rationally irrational to mute themselves.

3. In the long-run, creates track records that greatly enhance even casual observers' ability to discover reliable thinkers and dismiss unreliable thinkers.

Tyler's rebuttal has long been a variant on, "If you're so smart, why aren't you rich?" If you really know more than other people, you shouldn't waste your time making bets. You should take your knowledge to financial markets and make a killing. Anyone who fails to do so isn't really epistemically exceptional, no matter how many bets they've won.

For my part, I've always considered Tyler's reply quite weak. Rebuttal to his rebuttal: *Many* major intellectual issues simply aren't financially helpful to resolve. Suppose you could demonstrate that intelligent alien life exists in another galaxy. An amazing discovery, yet it's hard to see why financial markets would care in the slightest. This wouldn't be true, of course, if "Existence of intelligent alien life proven" securities existed, but they don't. Even the best-developed financial markets focus on a tiny sliver of logical space. Exchanges fret far more about pork bellies than life extension.[3] In any case, the world is so complex that you can *perfectly* understand a wide range of relevant issues but still go bankrupt investing on your knowledge. Suppose, for example, you knew *exactly* how much petroleum Earth contained. An amazing feat, but it's far from clear that you could make money off of this knowledge.

At this point, you might reply, "Knowledge of a few facts won't ensure riches. Still, anyone who knew *a lot* of important facts could easily become a billionaire." Plausible, but is it true?

I fear not. Consider this hypothetical: Back in March, you acquired *omniscient* foresight for all of the following variables: the GDP of every country on Earth; the unemployment rate of every country on Earth; total spending by country on consumption, investment, government purchases, transfers, exports, and imports in every country on Earth; and the true coronavirus infection and death rates. Suppose that, armed with this godlike knowledge, you tried to predict where international stock markets would stand today.

What would you have predicted?

Personally, I would have expected stock markets to fall by at least 2/3rds, and remain around that low level. I'm not alone, as this Twitter poll showed.[4]

In reality, global markets have almost fully recovered. With 20/20 hindsight, maybe this will make sense, but I remain utterly confused. What I do know, however, is that omniscient foresight about a long list of macroeconomic variables wouldn't have made me rich. Indeed, I could easily have lost *everything*; full of hubris in my god-like knowledge, I might have leveraged all my assets to short global markets. Only too late would I have found that *omniscience is not enough*. You can have flawless knowledge of the macroeconomy yet dangerously unreliable knowledge of the financial economy.

One could protest: "You could have made a killing if your omniscience extended to *specific firms*. Imagine if you perfectly foresaw how much people would start buying from Amazon." That sounds right, but reinforces my main point. Namely: The market poorly rewards deep, accurate knowledge of the Big Picture. If you want to get rich, you're better off knowing the right kinds of trivia.

Not convinced? Ask yourself: If you wanted to get rich, which would you rather know: *The release date for the first coronavirus vaccine — or the name of the company that discovers this vaccine?*

If you care about the Big Picture, *when* is obviously vastly more important than *who*. If you're looking for a mountain of gold, however, *who* is vastly more important than *when*.

Last question: Isn't it comically convenient for me to claim that I just-so-happen to have great knowledge of the Big Picture, but mediocre knowledge of how to become a billionaire? No, because the tournament to gain great knowledge of the Big Picture is *much* less competitive than the tournament to become a billionaire! The world is packed with brilliant people who desperately want to become fabulously rich. The quest to grasp the Big Picture, in contrast, is only a nerdy hobby. In a world where 10% of MIT and Caltech graduates devoted their lives and egos to public betting, my betting record would be lost in the shuffle. The reason I've excelled, in short, is that most of the thinkers able to outrun me neither know nor care that there's a race.

August 24, 2020

Notes

1. Caplan, Bryan. "Betting Rules." *EconLog,* February 11, 2016. Caplan, Bryan. "The Silence of the Bets." *EconLog,* July 8, 2013. Caplan, Bryan. "What a Bet Shows." *EconLog,* June 14, 2017.
2. Caplan, Bryan. "My Complete Bet Wiki." *EconLog,* January 2, 2020. Caplan, Bryan. "What Does the Betting Norm Tax?" *EconLog,* March 14, 2009.
3. Caplan, Bryan. "Life Extension: Economists vs. The Public." *EconLog,* September 10, 2023.
4. @bryan_caplan. "If the Dow had crashed to 10,000 in March..." *Twitter,* August 8, 2020.

Tranquility for A Dollar a Day:
An Open Letter to *Adbusters*

Dear *Adbusters*:[1]

 While your publication seems to have little use for neoclassical economics professors, there is at least one topic where you have my sympathy.[2] Like you, I find most advertising to be extremely painful. Commercial radio, with its shrill and mind-numbing sales pitches, is the worst. But the ads on t.v. are almost as bad.

 A couple years ago, however, I managed to eliminate 98% of the advertising-related aggravation in my life, and I'd like to share how I did it. While the following may seem flippant, I mean it in all seriousness. I freed myself from the pain of advertising by:

 1. Subscribing to XM Radio.[3] This product, available for $12.95/month, allows me to enjoy a fantastic variety of music, completely commercial-free. Unlike public radio, moreover, there are no excrutiating pledge drives.

 2. Getting a Digital Video Recorder (DVR) from Dish Network.[4] As long as I plan ahead, I can conveniently pre-

record any program I want to watch, then fast-forward through all commercials. It's not quite a good as not having commercials in the first place, but it's close. The cost: $4.98/month.

Admittedly, another downside of commercial television is that it tends to be bland and insipid, because bland and insipid gets ratings, which means advertising revenue. But the solution for this problem has been around for decades:

3. Subscribing to HBO.[5] For $13.99/month, you can watch high-quality programs with artistic integrity, like *The Sopranos* and *Rome*. Combined with a DVR, you get even more value, because you can pre-record everything worth watching.

The total monthly cost of tranquility: $31.92, or about a dollar a day. If you can afford the $35.00/year annual subscription fee to hear people complain about commercials in *Adbusters*, you can easily afford to pay a dollar a day to actually solve your problem.

My solution obviously does little to rid our whole culture of advertising. It is only an individual-level solution. But at minimum, my advice will significantly improve *your* life. Call it "corporate blackmail" if you must, but don't cut off your nose to spite your face.

Furthermore — and now the economist in me re-emerges — beyond the individual level, *the "problem" of advertising shouldn't be solved*. Hard as it is for me or you to fathom, many people don't mind — or actually like — commercials. When I visit my dad, he yells at me for muting them. As with religious disagreement, the best solution to commercial disagreement is live and let live.

Sincerely,
Prof. Bryan Caplan
Department of Economics
George Mason University

November 14, 2005

Notes

1. "Adbusters." *Adbusters.*
2. "Is Econ Just Politics in Disguise?" *Adbusters.*
3. "SiriusXM." *SiriusXM.*
4. "Dish Network." *Dish.*
5. "HBO." *HBO.*

Let Them Get Roommates

A fun fact about the U.S. versus Europe is that the poorest 25% of Americans have more living space than the average American.[1] But some Americans been left behind. Our most deprived citizens often sleep three to a room, eat prison-grade food, and share bathroom facilities with dozens of unhygenic strangers. They are known as...*college students*.

I know. I lived in a triple in the UC Berkeley dorms back in 90-91. I was the last guy to arrive, so naturally I got the top bunk. Not fun.

But who feels sorry for college students in a triple? No one, as best I can tell. They barely even feel sorry for themselves. They're just supposed to get used to it, to "suck it up," and they do. As long as they aren't contributing to society, they ought to concentrate on bettering themselves, not complain about the unfairness of it all.

A friend of mine who is a bishop in the Mormon Church tells me that before anyone can go on the church dole, they get a little advice from a Mormon financial planner. The planner

31

takes a good look at the lifestyle of the needy, and frequently concludes that frugal living, not financial assistance, is the right answer.

As Econlog's resident Non-Bleeding Heart Libertarian, this sensible Mormon practice suggests a hard-boiled question. Why aren't (relatively) poor Americans expected to live like college students?

To put it more concretely: Before anyone starts collecting welfare, it is more than fair to ask them — for starters — to try to solve their own problem by taking on some roommates. Is it beneath their dignity to live like college students? I think not.

While I'm stepping on some sensitivities, I may as well point out a nice side benefit. If you choose your roommates wisely, you don't need the government to subsidize daycare just to get single moms back in the labor force. You've got a ready-made baby-sitting coop right in your own home.[3] He probably doesn't want the credit, but I'd still like to thank Paul Krugman for the inspiration![4]

March 25, 2005

Notes

1. "Europe vs. America." *Opinion Journal*, June 20, 2004.
2. "Organizing a Babysitting Coop." *Essortment*, 2002.
3. Krugman, Paul. "How Fast Can the U.S. Economy Grow?" *Harvard Business Review*, 1997.

The Economics of the Gift of Life

I f someone gives another person $100, almost all economists agree that the recipient is better off. Hard-line neoclassical economists will say it's true by definition; the rest won't be so emphatic, but they'll confidently agree. Even happiness researchers will probably sign on; income doesn't raise happiness *much*, but the effect's still positive.

If someone gives another person the *gift of life*, however, I've noticed that many economists suddenly become agnostic. $100? Definitely an improvement. Being alive? Meh.

It's hard to see the logic. Why would a minor gift of cash be a clear-cut gain, but a massive gift of human capital be a question mark? In both cases, the recipient seems to have what economists call "free disposal" — a cheap, painless away of getting rid of the unwanted gift.[1] Don't want $100? Drop it on the sidewalk. Don't want to be alive? Drop yourself on the sidewalk. As the great Epicurus wrote:

Yet much worse still is the man who says it is good
not to be born, but "once born make haste to pass the

gates of Death." [Theognis, 427]

For if he says this from conviction why does he not pass away out of life? For it is open to him to do so, if he had firmly made up his mind to this. But if he speaks in jest, his words are idle among men who cannot receive them.[2]

You could object that suicide is a lot more painful than it looks. Yes, there are painless, effective ways to do away with yourself. But before you leap, you have to live with the knowledge that you're causing great pain to everyone who cares about you. If you'd never existed, you wouldn't be missed.

Once you accept this line of thinking, though, $100 could easily be a curse, too. Many people couldn't throw away $100 without feeling like idiots. And once they have the money, their standards of acceptable consumption might ratchet up so they actually need the gift to compensate.

Ultimately, though, skepticism about the value of either gift — $100 or life itself — seems implausible and forced. While it's *conceivable* that the recipient will wish his "benefactor" had left him alone, it's highly unlikely. As I quip in *Selfish Reasons to Have More Kids*, "No one asks to be born, but almost everyone would if he could." The same holds for sneaking $100 bills in stranger's pockets.

August 29, 2010

Notes

1. Caplan, Bryan. "Free Disposal." *EconLog*, October 10, 2007.
2. Epicurus. "Letter to Menoeceus." *MIT Classics.*

The Fallacy of Dulling
the Pain of Poverty

Why are the poor more likely to abuse drugs and alcohol? As a matter of dollars and cents, substance abuse should *rise*, not fall, with income.[1] These habits are expensive, both directly and indirectly. Directly: Drugs and alcohol cost money. Indirectly: Drug and alcohol abuse make you less employable, less healthy, more reckless, and more likely to get in trouble with the law.

First-hand accounts of poverty generally recognize that heavy users of drugs and alcohol pay a high material cost. Yet they rarely reach my verdict: that other factors — like low IQ, low conscientiousness, low patience, or plain irrationality — must be driving both poverty and substance abuse. Instead, observers usually say that the poor consume drugs and alcohol to "dull the pain." Some even argue that the poor are being entirely rational: If your life is a living hell, narcoticizing yourself is the simplest solution.

There's just one problem with this explanation: By almost all accounts, substance abuse *eventually* makes your life worse.

The long-term addict's life is utterly wretched — even if you average in his periodic drug-induced euphorias. Someone who has yet to start using drugs and alcohol doesn't face a choice between "full pain" and "dulled pain." Instead, he chooses between two paths of pain:

Path #1: Full pain in the short-run, followed by gradual life progress.

Path #2: Dulled pain in the short-run, followed by a gradual downward spiral into abject misery.

Suppose you're poor. Your life is unusually painful, so the *immediate* effect of drugs and alcohol is especially attractive.

The long-run prognosis for a poor substance abuser, however, is especially *repellent.* You hit "rock bottom" sooner because you don't have far to fall. And your version of "rock bottom" is extra bleak because you lack the financial resources and social connections to cushion the blow and get back on your feet.

The lesson: On net, poverty isn't a believable root cause of substance abuse, because being poor doesn't make substance abuse a better overall deal. Why then would poor people be more inclined to narcoticize themselves? Once again, we should look for root causes of poverty *and* pathology. Low patience is the most obvious suspect. If you loathe to defer gratification, you'll tend to have low income, and eagerly use drugs and alcohol today despite their awful cost down the line.

Closing questions: If *you* were poor, would you turn to drugs and alcohol? If you were a social worker, would you advise the poor to turn to drugs and alcohol? I doubt it. The reason, of course, is that on some level you already know what I'm telling you: Poverty is no excuse for substance abuse because substance abuse is an absurd response to poverty.

July 26, 2012

Notes

1. Caplan, Bryan. "Poverty and Behavior: Generalizing Yglesias", *EconLog*, July 25, 2012.

The Depression Preference

When I describe mental illness as "an extreme, so-cially disapproved preference," the most convincing counter-example people offer is depression.[1] Do I really think people "want to be depressed" or choose depression as a bizarre alternative lifestyle?

My quick answer: These objections confuse preferences with *meta*-preferences.

No one chooses to have the gene for cilantro aversion.[2] Yet people with the cilantro aversion gene are perfectly able to eat this vegetable. They just strongly *prefer* not to.

Similarly, when I say that alcoholics are people who value heavy consumption of alcoholic beverages more than family harmony, this doesn't mean that they *like* having these priorities. If they could press a button which would eliminate their craving for alcohol, I bet many alcoholics would press it. But given their actual cravings, they prefer to keep drinking heavily despite the suffering of their families.

The same holds even more strongly for the typical person diagnosed with clinical depression. Most people with loving families and successful careers are happy. Clinically depressed people, however, often have both loving families and successful careers, yet still want to kill themselves. Their preference is so extreme that it confuses the rest of us. They'd almost surely rather have a different preference. But it is their preference nonetheless.

Not convinced? Think back to the early 1970s, when psychiatrists still classified homosexuality as a mental disorder.[3] I object, "Mental disorder? No, it's just an extreme, socially disapproved preference." When critics incredulously respond, "Do you really think people choose to be gay?," I say they're confusing preferences with meta-preferences. To be gay is to sexually prefer people of your own gender. This doesn't mean that gays *want* to feel this way. If a gay-to-straight conversion button existed in the intolerant world of 1960, I bet that most gays would have gladly pushed it for themselves. Even today, I think many gay teens would press the conversion button to fit in and avoid conflict. But so what? Hypothetical buttons can't transform a preference into a disorder.

Is this all just a word game? No. The economic distinction between preferences and constraints that I'm drawing upon has three big substantive implications here.

First, people with extreme preferences *could* make different choices. People with cilantro aversion are able to eat cilantro. Alcoholics are able to stop drinking. The depressed can refrain from suicide. And so on. This is fundamentally different from my inability to bench press 300 pounds — or live to be 150 years old.

Second, as a corollary, people with extreme preferences can — and routinely do — respond to incentives.[4] People with cilantro aversion are more likely to eat cilantro if other foods are expensive or inconvenient. Alcoholics respond to alcohol taxes — and family pressure. Depressed parents may delay suicide until their kids are grown. Even in a tragic situation, incentives matter.*

Third, as a further corollary, people with extreme preferences can — and routinely do — find better ways to cope. People reshape their own preferences all the time; perhaps you can do the same. Failing that, perhaps you can discover more constructive ways to satisfy the preferences that you're stuck with. For example, if you're extremely depressed despite great career success, you really should try some experiments in living. Perhaps you'll be miserable whatever you do. But if you've only experienced one narrow lifestyle, *how do you know*? Maybe you'd feel better if you tried putting friendship or hobbies above "achievement."

It's tempting to insist that there's something pathological about having conflicting preferences and meta-preferences. On reflection, however, these conflicts are a ubiquitous feature of human existence. Almost everyone would like to feel differently in some important dimension. Almost everyone reading this probably wishes they were less lazy, more patient, more outgoing, more loving, more ambitious, or more persistent. But you still are the preferences you really have. There's plenty of room for improvement, but that doesn't mean you're sick.

* I'm well-aware that many physical symptoms also respond to incentives. You can pressure a diabetic to lose weight, which in turn reverses his diabetes. But all of these incentive effects require *time* to work. The symptoms of mental illness, in contrast, can and often do respond to incentives *instantly*, because they are choices that are always within your grasp. "I'm divorcing you unless you stop drink-

ing right now" is a viable threat. "I'm divorcing you unless you stop being diabetic right now" is silly one.

March 26, 2019

Notes

1. Caplan, Bryan. "The Economics of Szasz: Preferences, Constraints, and Mental Illness." *Rationality and Society*, 2006.
2. Callaway, Ewen. "Soapy Taste of Coriander Linked to Genetic Variants." *Nature*, September 12, 2012.
3. Caplan, Bryan. "ADHD Reconsidered." *EconLog*, February 2, 2016.
4. "Incentives." *EconLib Guides*.

How I Raised My Social Intelligence

M y social intelligence is a lot higher than it used to be. I still wouldn't say that I'm "good with people." But in my youth, I was truly inept. In junior high, I had one real friend, and many overt enemies. Since then, I've at least managed to claw my way up to mediocrity.

A lot of social intelligence is in details and practice. If I could travel back in time and spend five minutes advising myself, though, here are the principles I would try to teach myself.

1. *Good conversation is an exchange.* The most basic form of social ineptitude is to say what's on your mind, even though you have no reason to believe your listeners are interested. Even more cloddish: Saying what's on your mind, even though you know that your listeners are not interested. In a useful conversation, in contrast, there is a double coincidence of wants.[1] You have to be interested in what I have to say; I have to be interested in what you have to say. This is an important reason why people with conventional interests seem more socially intelligent. Even if they don't check whether their

audience cares, it probably does.

I imagine that my teenage self would immediately object, "But *no one*'s interested in what I have to say." My two replies: (a) If that's true, it's still better to keep your thoughts to yourself than antagonize people you're going to see repeatedly. (b) People will be much more interested in your thoughts if you make marginal adjustments in topics and presentation.

2. *Be friendly.* It's not just good advice for libertarians; it's good advice for people.[2] A strong presumption in favor of kindness and respect almost never hurts you, and often helps you. Note that I say "presumption." Don't "wait and see" if people deserve friendly treatment. Hand it out first, no questions asked. You will make friends (very good), avoid making enemies (good), and occasionally show undeserved kindness and respect (only mildly bad).

3. *Keeping friends is more important than getting your way.* You should think twice before asking anyone for help. If you still think it's a good idea, try to make your request easy to refuse. "How would you feel about..." is much better than "Please, please just do me this one favor!" In the short-run, of course, the pushy approach is often effective. But life is a repeated game, pushing leads to resentment, and your relationships are more valuable than almost any specific victory.

The world often perceives economists as low in social intelligence. Maybe we are, but there's no reason for it to be that way. The insight that good conversation is an exchange should come naturally to the economically literate. A policy of blanket friendliness ought to make sense to anyone familiar with weakly dominant strategies.[3] And once you realize that asking for help is an implicit intertemporal trade, the wisdom of restraint and delicacy is easy to see.

Admittedly, if your social intelligence has always been high, my recommendations will strike you as obvious. If they're so obvious, though, why do so many smart people act like don't know them?

June 17, 2009

Notes

1. "Coincidence of Wants." *Wikipedia.*
2. Caplan, Bryan. "The Case for Libertarian Friendliness." *EconLog,* July 14, 2008.
3. "Weakly Dominant Strategy." *GameTheory.*

Part II

Life Hacks

My Beautiful Bubble

U nlike many readers of *Coming Apart*, you don't have to convince me that I live in a Bubble.[1] I've known it for decades. In fact, I think my 3-out-of-20 score on the "How Thick Is Your Bubble?" quiz greatly *over*states my integration into American society.[2] I live in a Bubble Within a Bubble.

You might even call it my Imaginary Charter City.[3] I'm not just surrounded by Ph.D.s; I'm surrounded by libertarian economics Ph.D.s. I'm not just unfamiliar with NASCAR; I forget the very existence of professional sports for months at a time. I don't just watch shows for yuppies; I manage my entertainment to make sure that I never hear a commercial.[4] In my world, Alex Tabarrok is more important than Barack Obama, Robin Hanson is more important than Paul Krugman, and the late Gary Gygax is more important than Jeremy Lin... whoever that might be.

Unlike most American elites, I don't feel the least bit bad about living in a Bubble. I share none of their egalitarian or nationalist scruples. Indeed, I've wanted to live in a Bubble for as long as I can remember. Since childhood, I've struggled to psychologically and socially wall myself off from "my" society. At 40, I can fairly say, "Mission accomplished."[5]

Why put so much distance between myself and the outside world? Because despite my legendary optimism, I find my society unacceptable.[6] It is dreary, insipid, ugly, boring, wrong, and wicked. Trying to reform it is largely futile; as the Smiths tell us, "The world won't listen."[7] Instead, I pursue the strategy that actually works: Making my small corner of the world beautiful in my eyes. If you ever meet my children or see my office, you'll know what I mean.

I'm hardly autarchic. I import almost everything I consume from the outside world. Indeed, I frequently leave the security of my Bubble to walk the earth. But I do so as a tourist. Like a truffle pig, I hunt for the best that "my" society has to offer. I partake. Then I go back to my Bubble and tell myself, "America's a nice place to visit, but you wouldn't want to live there."

Many people will find my attitude repugnant. They shouldn't. Yes, I step to the beat of my own drummer. But I'm not trying to push my lifestyle on others. I don't pester people who identify with America as it is. Indeed, I wish outsiders the best of luck. My only request: If you're not happy with your world, don't try to pop my beautiful Bubble. Either fix your world, or get to work and make a beautiful Bubble of your own.

March 8, 2012

Notes

1. Caplan, Bryan. "An Optimist's Take on Charles Murray's *Coming Apart.*" *EconLog*, January 17, 2012.
2. "Do You Live in a Bubble Quiz." *PBS*, March 24, 2016.
3. Caplan, Bryan. "A Quick Case for Charter Cities: Memo to the Gates Foundation." *EconLog*, March 22, 2011.
4. Caplan, Bryan. "Tranquility for A Dollar a Day: An Open Letter to *Adbusters.*" *EconLog*, March 22, 2011.
5. Caplan, Bryan. "40 Things I Learned in My First 40 Years." *EconLog*, April 8, 2011.
6. Caplan, Bryan. "The Cynical Optimist." *EconLog*, September 17, 2005.
7. "The World Won't Listen." *Wikipedia.*

Make Your Own Bubble
in 10 Easy Steps

Someone on Twitter asked for advice on how to create a Beautiful Bubble.[1] Perhaps he was teasing me, but it's a good question. Here's my 10 Step Program:

1. Amicably divorce your society. Don't get angry at the strangers who surround you, just accept the fact that you're not right for each other.

2. Stop paying attention to things that aggravate you unless (a) they *concretely* affect your life AND (b) you can realistically do something about them. Start by ceasing to follow national and world news.

3. Pay *less frequent* attention to things that aggravate you even if they *do* concretely affect your life and you *can* realistically do something about them. For example, if you check your email twenty times a day and find the experience frustrating, try cutting back to two or three times a day. If you need to know about world politics, read history books, not newspaper articles.

4. Emotionally distance yourself from people you personally

know who aggravate you. Don't purge anyone — that causes more trouble than it saves. Just accept the fact that you aren't going to change them.

5. Abandon your First World Problems mentality.[2] Consciously compare your income to Haitian poverty, your health status to Locked-In Syndrome, your sorrow to that of a parent who has lost a child.[3] As Tsunami Bomb tells us, "Be grateful that you have a brain for thinking/ And legs to take you places." For guidance, repeatedly read Epicurus' *Letter to Menoeceus* and Julian Simon's *Good Mood*.[4]

6. Now that you have emptied your life of frustration, you are ready to fill it with joy. Start doing things that make you happy even — nay, especially — if most people in your ex-society disrespect them. Spend $1 a day to filter out annoying advertising and intrusion.[5]

7. Actively try to make more friends with people who share your likes. In the Internet age, this is shockingly easy. *Don't* try to make more friends who share your *dis*likes. You should build friendship on common passions, not joint contempt.

8. Find a career you really enjoy. Ask yourself, "Will I take daily pride in this work?" and "Are the kind of people I want to befriend statistically over-represented in this line of work?" If you have to signal for years to get this job, sigh, signal, and see Step 5.[6]

9. If you're single, stop dating outside of your sub-sub culture. Happy relationships are based on shared values and mutual admiration so intense that outsiders laugh. Let them laugh.

10. Now that your own life is in order, you are emotionally ready to quixotically visit your ex-society. Maybe you want to

publicly argue for open borders, abolition of the minimum wage, or pacifism.[7] Go for it. Bend over backwards to be friendly.[8] Take pride in your quixotic quest. Then go home to your Beautiful Bubble and relax.

Coda: Many perpetually aggravated people tell me they "just can't" adopt my advice. Perhaps they're right to think that they can't follow my advice 100%. But so what? Anyone can adopt my advice *at the margin*. Why not spend one extra hour a day in your Bubble and see what happens?

April 11, 2013

Notes

1. Caplan, Bryan. "My Beautiful Bubble." *EconLog*, March 9, 2012.
2. "First World Problems." *QuickMeme.*
3. "Locked-In Syndrome." *Wikipedia.*
4. Epicurus. "Letter to Menoeceus." *MIT Classics.* Simon, Julian. *Good Mood.* 1999.
5. Caplan, Bryan. "Tranquility for a Dollar a Day: An Open Letter to Adbusters." *EconLog*, November 14, 2005.
6. Caplan, Bryan. "The Magic of Education." *EconLog*, November 28, 2011.
7. Caplan, Bryan. "Why Should We Restrict Immigration?" *Cato Journal*, 2012. Caplan, Bryan. "The Myopic Empiricism of the Minimum Wage." *EconLog*, March 12, 2013.

Caplan, Bryan. "The Common-Sense Case for Pacifism." *EconLog*, April 5, 2010.

8. Caplan, Bryan. "The Case for Libertarian Friendliness." *EconLog*, July 14, 2008.

Shy Male Nerds
and the Bubble Strategy

S cott Alexander keeps writing intellectually powerful critiques of radical feminism's War on Shy Male Nerds (SMNs).[1] His latest:

> When feminists say that the market failure for young women is caused by slut-shaming, I stop slut-shaming, and so do most other decent people. When men say that the market failure for young men is caused by nerd-shaming, feminists write dozens of very popular articles called things like "On Nerd Entitlement".

> The reason that my better nature thinks that it's irrelevant whether or not Penny's experience growing up was better or worse than Aaronson's: when someone tells you that something you are doing is making their life miserable, you don't lecture them about how your life is worse, even if it's true. You STOP DOING IT.[2]

[Quick aside: In high school, I definitely fit the SMN profile. I played Dungeons and Dragons with my male friends every Saturday night, and did not go to prom. By my second year of college, however, the problem ceased to be personally relevant. I met my wife when I was 19, married at 23, and we just celebrated our 20th anniversary. My experience may color my advice, but I leave readers to decide if that's a bug or a feature.]

My main question when reading Scott's defense of SMNs: Is this really the best way to help them out? Sure, some SMNs may feel better after reading Scott. But Scott's main intended audience seems to be the feminists who mistreat SMNs. And frankly, I can't imagine even Scott's earnest voice changing their minds. In fact, even Scott seems extremely pessimistic. He even ends his conclusion with a disclamer:

> I already know that there are people reading this planning to write responses with titles like "Entitled Blogger Says All Women Exist For His Personal Sexual Pleasure, Also Men Are More Oppressed Than Women, Also Nerds Are More Oppressed Than WWII Era Jews".

If helping SMNs is the goal, I think I know a better way. As usual, I recommend self-help. Specifically: SMNs should exclude hostile feminists from their Bubble.[3] Stop arguing with hostile feminists. Stop reading them. If you know any in real life, stop associating with them. Even if they have halfway decent reasons for berating you, you're clearly not right for each other. The best response is to amicably go your separate ways.[4]

I realize that this approach does not solve the deeper problem of SMN loneliness. But that's no reason to amplify your unhappiness with unpleasant, fruitless social interaction with people who emotionally abuse you.

January 2, 2015

Notes

1. Alexander, Scott. "Radicalizing the Romanceless." *Slate Star Codex,* August 31, 2014.
2. Alexander, Scott. "Untitled." *Slate Star Codex*, January 1, 2015.
3. Caplan, Bryan. "Make Your Own Bubble in 10 Easy Steps." *EconLog*, April 11, 2013. Caplan, Bryan. "My Beautiful Bubble." *EconLog*, March 9, 2012.
4. Caplan, Bryan. "The Futility of Quarreling When There is No Surplus to Divide." *EconLog*, February 11, 2014.

Two Heuristics to Live By When You Don't Know What You're Doing

When we see people making bad decisions — whether as consumers or voters — we often blame the "complexity" of the issues they face. If Ph.D. economists can't figure out the best mortgage to use, how can we expect the average borrower to do so? If health policy experts can't agree on how to fix the U.S. medical system, what is the typical voter to think?

But if complexity is your only demon, I've got two simple rules of thumb to exorcise him. Here goes:

1. If you don't have clear and convincing evidence that doing something is better than doing nothing, do nothing.

2. If you know that doing nothing is bad, but don't have clear and convincing evidence that one action is better than another, do the simplest, standard thing.

I frequently apply these rules to my consumption decisions. Until I'm convinced that a product will make my life better, I just don't buy it. I might enjoy a big plasma T.V., but until a seller clearly explains how he's going to painlessly install it in my house, I'm not buying one. If I do decide in favor of a plasma T.V., but remain confused about which one to buy, I'll probably just get the biggest one that CostCo carries.

In the mortgage market, similarly, my heuristics say: (a) Rent until it's clear that buying will improve your life; and (b) Get a standard 30-year fixed-rate mortgage from an established lender. Don't buy a house you might not be able to afford by signing a contract you can't explain to your friends.

Needless to say, voters could also use these heuristics to decide which policies to support. Until there's clear and convincing evidence that healthcare reform or invading someone will make things better, you're better off saying No. And if you *are* convinced that "doing something" is better than "doing nothing," your best bet is to go with the simplest, standard option.

Admittedly, that last sentence of advice makes me a little uncomfortable. Many policies I detest — like immigration restrictions — are nevertheless simple and standard.[1] But overall, I'm not too worried about the political consequences of my rules of thumb. If voters just learned to say No until a politician could clearly show that government action would improve the world, voters would shout down most of the policies I detest before they ever got to my second heuristic.

July 14, 2008

Notes

1. Caplan, Bryan. "Immigration Restrictions: A Solution in

Search of a Problem." *The Economist,* June 22, 2007.

More Bang for Your Buck; or, Better Ways to Buy Your Happiness

Money has little effect on happiness.[1] Ancient Greeks like Epicurus said it, and modern empirical psychology confirms it.[2] Why do we have so much trouble accepting this? In part, because our *immediate* reaction to money is highly favorable — and that sticks in our minds. Before long, however, hedonic adaptation kicks in.[3] We start to take our good fortune for granted... and then we largely forget that our fortune is good.

But there's probably another important reason why we have so much trouble accepting the weak effect of money on happiness. Namely: *There are so many ways to buy happiness with money!* The fact that "Money *doesn't* buy happiness" clashes with the equally obvious fact that "Money *can* buy happiness." The simplest reconciliation, of course, is that most people spend their money poorly. And in my experience, this reconciliation is entirely correct. Most people stubbornly spend lots of money on hedonic dead-ends, while ignoring omnipresent opportunities to turn cash into smiles.

So what are these alleged "omnipresent opportunities"? Here are my top picks.

1. Buy your way out of unpleasant chores by hiring other people to do them for you. Start with cleaning, laundry, yardwork, auto repair, childcare, and tax preparation.

2. Buy your way out of unpleasant chores by buying *different* products. Most obviously, switch to disposable plates, cups, and utensils. It's very cheap, and saves lots of time. If this gives you environmental guilt, compensate with some Effective Altruism.[4]

3. The leading source of happiness is pleasant social interaction. Use money to get more of it — and make your interaction more pleasant. If you have to spend hours preparing for and cleaning up for any gathering, you probably won't enjoy it much. So cut down on both preparation and cleanup using #1 and #2.

4. Don't buy products to impress strangers or casual acquaintances. They're barely paying any attention to you anyway.[5] Indeed, even your close friends probably don't pay that much attention to the details of your possessions. So if you and your immediate family won't durably enjoy an expensive product (such as... granite countertops), save your money.

5. Entertainment spending is one of the best ways to convert money into happiness. That's why they call it "entertainment."

6. If you live with other people, soundproof your house—especially if you have kids. Other people's music, t.v., and phone conversations (not to mention children's crying) don't just get on your nerves; they create needless conflict. But you don't have to choose between isolation and serenity. Solid wood doors aren't exactly cheap, but they're affordable.

7. Put less effort into finding a job that pays better than your current job. Put more effort into finding a job that is more enjoyable than your current job. First and foremost: Look for jobs with lots of pleasant social interaction.

Overarching doubt: Won't these attitudes alienate more conventional people? My answer: Only mildly, as long as you're friendly. *So be friendly*! And don't forget that these attitudes also attract people who are *eager* to actually enjoy life.

Finally: You can and should use your money to build and maintain your Beautiful Bubble![6]

<u>Update:</u> Keller Scholl rightly points out that I should have mentioned, "Spend money to cut your commuting time."

April 15, 2019

Notes

1. Caplan, Bryan. "Why I'm an Economic Optimist but Happiness Pessimist." *EconLog,* April 3, 2019.
2. Epicurus. "Letter to Menoeceus." *MIT Classics.*
3. Caplan, Bryan. "Happiness Research: Get Used to It." *EconLog,* March 1, 2006.
4. "Give Well." *GiveWell.*
5. Caplan, Bryan. "Get Over Yourself." *EconLog,* May 26, 2015.
6. Caplan, Bryan. "Make Your Own Bubble in 10 Easy Steps." *EconLog,* April 11, 2013.

What a Bet Shows

Whenever I win a bet, critics rush to say, "This doesn't prove you know better than me." They're right: Bets "prove" nothing. But that's a silly standard. For empirical questions, definitive proof is unavailable, so we have to settle for degrees of probability.

By this reasonable measure, how probative are bets? Taken individually, most bets are only marginally so. Even if one side offers 1000:1 odds and loses, this might only show that the loser was a fool to offer such great odds, not that his position on the underlying issue is flat wrong.

When we move from solitary bets to betting *records*, however, bets are telling indeed. A guy who wins one bet could easily have gotten lucky. But someone who wins 10 out of 10 bets — or, in my case, 14 out of 14 bets — almost certainly has superior knowledge and judgment.[1] This is especially true if someone lives the Bettors' Oath by credibly promising to bet on (or retract) *any* public statement.[2] A bet is a lot like a tennis match: one victory slightly raises the probability that the winner is the superior player, but it's entirely possible that he just got lucky. A betting *record*, in contrast, is a lot like a tennis *ranking*; people who win consistently against any challenger do so by skill, not luck.

After losing our unemployment bet, Tyler Cowen objected that betting:

> ...produces a celebratory mindset in the victor. That lowers the quality of dialogue and also introspection, just as political campaigns lower the quality of various ideas — too much emphasis on the candidates and the competition.[3]

Tyler's gets very close to the truth, but misses the most important lesson. Namely: In a busy world, ranking people by accuracy is not only helpful in the search for truth, but vital. No one has time to listen to more than a fraction of the armies of talking heads, or the memory to recall more than a fraction of their arguments. If we want to know the future as well as we're able, we need to identify people with good judgment — and ignore people with bad judgment. The first step, of course, is to unfollow pundits who refuse to put their money where their mouths are. We should take them as seriously as self-proclaimed tennis "champions" who've never publicly played a match.

June 14, 2017

Notes

1. Caplan, Bryan. "My Complete Bet Inventory: 2016 Edition." *EconLog*, April 19, 2016.
2. Caplan, Bryan. "The Bettor's Oath." *EconLog,* May 5, 2012.
3. Caplan, Bryan. "I Win My Long-Term Unemployment Bet with Tyler." *EconLog*, February 8, 2016. Cowen, Tyler. "The Employment to Population Ratio, Revisted." *Marginal Revolution,* February 9, 2016.

A Bettor's Tale

H ere's a great yarn of betting and political irrationality courtesy of EconLog reader Mathieu Giroux (used with his permission).[1]

My Uncle, like the vast majority of people living in North America, is not a fan of the idea of open borders. In fact, he's vehemently opposed. The first time I told him I favored the idea, his reaction was, well, a very hard to forget combination of incredulity and indignation. Free trade in goods was fine he maintained but to extend the idea to labor... madness! We would debate the issue via e-mail and when we saw each other in person. During one such visit, he was telling me, as he had repeatedly, that support for open borders was just one hell of an out there idea. I normally responded by saying that an idea being outside the mainstream hardly meant it was a bad idea. After all, support for many things that are now sacrosanct in our culture once only enjoyed the support of a few articulate radicals.

However, at that moment, a different response came to mind. I knew that the *Wall Street Journal* had editorialized in favor of open borders under Robert Bartley. My Uncle, a fiscal conservative who works in the financial sector, surely could not deny that the *Wall Street Journal* was an impeccably mainstream publication. So I said "Is the *Wall Street Journal* crazy? It has editorialized in favor of open borders." He did not believe that the *Journal* would ever be so "out there." Knowing I was right, and inspired by Bryan, I suggested we bet to settle the dispute.

The terms were clear: 50 bucks would be owed to me if I could find an editorial by the *Journal* calling for open borders and 50 owed to him if I couldn't. A 30 second Google search later and there it was: an editorial by the *Wall Street Journal* endorsing my ultra-marginal, insane libertarian notion of open borders. The editorial even used the term "open borders." My uncle was not happy. "This is from the 80s," he protested. "Did I say it was written yesterday? Come on Bob, the terms of the bet were clear. Any editorial from the *Journal* advocating this and you owe me $50."

I really didn't feel this was sneaky since it's not like the *Journal* has ever repudiated or even distanced itself from this position and has indeed written many editorials advocating policies consistent with the goal of ultimately opening up borders completely. A few minutes later, I was 50 dollars richer and he was 50 dollars poorer. Since then, I have routinely suggested betting to settle disputes.

No one else has agreed to bet which shows that even belligerent partisans back off when there is a cost to being wrong.

Oh and in all fairness to my Uncle, he's a very bright, pleasant, and successful guy. I hope to be like him in many ways, but, you know, without being terribly wrong on hugely important moral issues.

P.S. I'd add that Mathieu's uncle is praiseworthy for betting in the first place. As I've pledged before, "When I win a bet, I will not shame my opponent, for a betting loser has far more honor than the mass of men who live by loose and idle talk."[2]

March 27, 2015

Notes

1. Caplan, Bryan. "The Silence of the Bets." *Econ-Log*, July 8, 2013.   Caplan, Bryan. "Week 10: Ignorance, Irrationality, and Aggregation: Theory and Evidence. *Econ 854: Public Choice II (Graduate)*.
2. Caplan, Bryan. "The Bettor's Oath." *EconLog*, May 5, 2012.

Exposure Therapy:
When Probabilities Fail

I n chapter 4 of *Selfish Reasons to Have More Kids*, I show that — objectively speaking — kids today are safer than ever.[1] And I'm far from the first social scientist to point out the public's systematically biased beliefs about risk — try Aaron Wildavsky, Kip Viscusi, Cass Sunstein, or Levitt and Dubner.[2] One fact that we quants tend to overlook, unfortunately, is that many people still *feel* extremely afraid even after they accept the facts. This doesn't mean that correcting misconceptions is useless — many people's fear *does* respond to facts. But it does leave a tough question: What can we do for everyone else?

I'm pleased to report that an effective supplement to objective risk analysis exists. It's called *exposure therapy*. Psychologists use it to help people with severe anxiety problems — people who have nothing to fear but fear itself. The best source I've found is the *Handbook of Exposure Therapies*.[3] Intuitively, the idea is to get people to "face their fears." From the introductory chapter: "Exposure therapy... involves deliberate and planned exposure to a feared stimulus, or representation of the

stimulus, until the intensity of the person's distress recedes…"
The basic steps:

1. Choose to vividly experience a disturbing but tolerable fear. Depending on the fear, this means either first-hand experience (e.g. spiders), or detailed imagination (e.g. the kidnapping of your child). "Regardless of the way exposure therapy is conducted, clients are encouraged to confront their fears in the present-tense. For example, a client recounting a traumatic event in exposure therapy is encouraged to describe the event as if it were being relived."

2. Continue doing #1 until the experience or imagination has become less frightening.

3. Move on to more intense anxieties and repeat.

The *Handbook* also reviews clinical evidence on exposure therapy vs. other talk therapies vs. drugs vs. nothing vs. combinations of the above. The contributors to this volume are obviously sympathetic to exposure therapy, but their survey of the evidence is still impressive. In almost every case, they conclude that exposure therapy plus X is no better than — and often worse than — exposure therapy alone. The zero or negative marginal benefit of drugs is awfully Hansonian:

> With respect to short-run efficacy, a number of studies suggest that [some drugs] may enhance the effects of exposure-based CBT [cognitive-behavioral therapy]. However, an approximately equal number of clinical trials provide no support for this conclusion, and a meta-analysis of this literature indicates that combined treatment is no more effective than CBT alone… On the other hand, clinical trials have consistently failed to support an advantage

of combined treatment when long-term outcomes are considered. In fact, the two largest and most well-designed trials of combined treatments provide unambiguous evidence that pharmacotherapy... interferes with the durability of exposure-based CBT.

Does this mean that teaching probabilities is a waste of time? Not at all. Many people's anxiety *does* respond to objective information. But even if your anxiety is more stubborn, it's still good to learn about probabilities. If the sky really *is* falling, you should run for cover. But if the sky *isn't* falling, the best way to feel better is to sit down under the open sky and face your fear.

P.S. How can a Szaszian take this stuff seriously?[7] Easily. Szasz would deny that anxiety disorders are a "disease." But he'd surely admit that extreme fear of minor risks is a "problem in living" — and there's nothing anti-Szaszian about carefully comparing different strategies for overcoming such problems.

November 11, 2009

Notes

1. Caplan, Bryan. "Modernity as a Children's Paradise." *EconLog*, August 7, 2009.
2. Douglas, Mary and Aaron Wildavksy. *Risk and Culture: An Essay on the Selection of Technological and Environmental Dangers*, 1983. Viscusi, Kip. *The Value of Risks to Life and Health*, 1993. Sunstein, Cass. *Risk and Reason:*

Law, and the Environment, 2004. Caplan, Bryan. "The High Points of *Superfreakonomics*." *EconLog*, October 15, 2009.

3. Richard, David and Dean Lauterbach. *Handbook of Exposure Therapies*, 2006.

4. Caplan, Bryan. "The Economics of Szasz: Preferences, Constraints, and Mental Illness." *Rationality and Society*, 2006.

Is the Econ Ph.D. a Free Lunch?

Whie you're earning a Ph.D. in economics, you learn two big lessons:

1. There's no such thing as a free lunch.
2. You are in serious pain.

On reflection, though, I've decided that both of these lessons fall short of the truth. In fact, a Ph.D. in economics is, relative to other graduate degrees, an amazing deal. It's not literally a free lunch, but it is a heavily discounted lunch. Consider:

1. *What other Ph.D. can you realistically finish in 4 years?* People in other fields routinely take six or eight years to get their degrees. Most economists don't finish in 4 years, but it's quite do-able.

2. *What other Ph.D. can you earn without previous familiarity with the field?* Ph.D.-level econ is so different from undergraduate econ that it isn't that much of a handicap to start from scratch. You do of course need to know a fair amount of math, but you could have learned that math studying dozens of other fields.

3. *What other profession gives you so much freedom to choose*

your research topics? Many economists now devote their careers to studying topics that an outsider would classify as political science, psychology, or sociology. Some economists even do work that basically amounts to history or philosophy, though they probably need to work on more conventional topics until they get tenure.

4. *What other Ph.D. has such a great safety net?* A Ph.D. in philosophy (not redundant, though it seems so) who fails to become a professor of philosophy has few good alternatives. An econ Ph.D. who fails to become an econ professor can become an economic consultant and make big money.

5. *The pain of the econ Ph.D. is not all that bad.* Yes, it hurts at the time. But the key question too many grad students in econ — including me! — lose sight of is: Compared to what? Does it hurt more to be an econ Ph.D. than a Ph.D. in math? History? Classics? Does it hurt compared to a real job? I think not.

Overall, the econ Ph.D. is such a good deal that I would seriously advise people who want to do research in political science, psychology, or even history to just get an econ Ph.D. and become a professor of economics. Even if you have to research topics you don't care about until you get tenure (and you probably won't have to), you could easily earn tenure in econ before you would have defended your dissertation in another field.

Needless to say, it's not really in my interest for my field to be flooded by the best students in political science, psychology, history, and beyond. But — besides giving me the opportunity to do the work I love, with reasonable material comfort, and zero job stress — what's my field ever done for me?

October 15, 2005

Being Single Is a Luxury

I'm baffled by people who blame declining marriage rates on poverty. Why? *Because being single is more expensive than being married.* Picture two singles living seperately. If they marry, they sharply cut their total housing costs. They cut the total cost of furniture, appliances, fuel, and health insurance. Even groceries get cheaper: think CostCo.

These savings are especially blatant when your income is low. Even the official poverty line acknowledges them.[1] The Poverty Threshold for a household with one adult is $11,139; the Poverty Threshold for a household with two adults is $14,218. When two individuals at the poverty line maintain separate households, they're effectively spending 2*$11,139-$14,218=$8,060 a year to stay single.

But wait, there's more. Marriage doesn't just cut expenses. It raises couples' income.[2] In the NLSY, married men earn about 40% more than comparable single men; married women earn about 10% less than comparable single women. From a couples' point of view, that's a big net bonus. And much of this bonus seems to be causal.[3]

If you're rich, admittedly, you have to consider the marriage tax.[4] But weighed against all the financial benefits of marriage, it's usually only a modest drawback.

Yes, you can capture some these benefits simply by cohabitating. But hardly all. And cohabitation is far less stable than marriage.[5] Long-term joint investments — like buying a house — are a lot more likely to blow up in your face. And while there may be some male cohabitation premium, it's smaller than the marriage premium.[6]

If being single is so expensive, why are the poor far less likely to get married and stay married? I'm sure you could come up with a stilted neoclassical explanation. But this is yet another case where behavioral economics and personality psychology have a better story.[7] Namely: Some people are extremely impulsive and short-sighted. If you're one of them, you tend to mess up your life in every way. You don't invest in your career, and you don't invest in your relationships. You take advantage of your boss and co-workers, and you take advantage of your romantic partners. You refuse to swallow your pride — to admit that the best job and the best spouse you can get, though far from ideal, are much better than nothing. Your behavior feels good at the time. But in the long-run people see you for what you are, and you end up poor and alone.

February 8, 2012

Notes

1. "Poverty Thresholds." *US Census.*

2. Caplan, Bryan. "The College Premium vs. the Marriage Premium: A Case of Double Standards." *EconLog*, January 23, 2012.
3. Ginther, Donna and Madeline Zavodny. "Is The Marriage Premium Due To Selection? The Effect of Shotgun Weddings on the Return to Marriage." *Journal of Population Economics*, 2001.
4. "Marriage Penalty." *Wikipedia.*
5. "Cohabitation Premium." *Google Scholar.*
6. Mamun, Arif. "Is There a Cohabitation Premium in Men's Earnings? *SSRN*, 2004.
7. Beaulier, Scott. "Behavioral Economics and Perverse Effects of the Welfare State." *Kyklos,* 2007. Caplan, Bryan. "Poverty, Conscientiousness, and Broken Families." *EconLog*, November 1, 2011.

What's Really Wrong With Cryonics

I don't want to achieve immortality through my work. I want to achieve it through not dying.

— Woody Allen

One of the most engaging after-lunch conversations of my life was when Robin Hanson sat me down and gave me the cryonics version of the Drake Equation.[1] The Drake Equation multiplies seven variables together in order to calculate the number of civilizations in our galaxy with which communication is possible. The Hanson Equation, similarly, multiplies a bunch of factors together in order to calculate how many expected years of life you will gain by signing a contract to freeze your head when you die.

During his presentation, I noticed that Robin spent almost all of his time on various scientific sub-disciplines and the trajectory of their progress. On these matters, I was fairly willing to defer to his superior knowledge (with the caveat that perhaps his enthusiasm was carrying him away). What disturbed me was when I realized how low he set his threshold for success. Robin didn't care about biological survival. He didn't need his brain implanted in a cloned body. He just wanted his neurons preserved well enough to "upload himself" into a computer.

To my mind, it was ridiculously easy to prove that "uploading yourself" isn't life extension. "An upload is merely a simulation. It wouldn't be you," I remarked. "It would if the simulation were accurate enough," he told me.

I thought I had him trapped. "Suppose we uploaded you while you were still alive. Are you saying that if someone blew your biological head off with a shotgun, you'd still be alive?!" Robin didn't even blink: "I'd say that I just *got smaller*."

The more I furrowed my brow, the more earnestly he spoke. "It all depends on what you choose to define as you," he finally declared. I said: "But that's a circular definition. Illogical!" He didn't much care.

Then I attacked him from a different angle. If I'm whatever I define as me, why bother with cryonics? Why not "define myself" as my Y-chromosome, or my writings, or the human race, or carbon? By Robin's standard, all it takes to vastly extend your life is to identify yourself with something highly durable.

His reply: "There are limits to what you can choose to identify with." I was dumbstruck at the time. But now I'd like to ask him, "OK, then why don't you spend more time trying to overcome your limited ability to identify with durable things? Maybe psychiatric drugs or brain surgery would do the trick."

I'd like to think that Robin's an outlier among cryonics advocates, but in my experience, he's perfectly typical. Fascination with technology crowds out not just philosophy of mind, but common sense.[2] My latest cryonics encounter was especially memorable. When I repeated my standard objections, the advocate flatly replied, "Those aren't interesting questions." *Not interesting questions*?! They're common sense, and they go to the heart of the cryonic dream.

Personally, I'd really like to live forever — in the normal English sense of the phrase "live forever." I wish cryonics could realistically offer me that. Unfortunately, the sophistry of its advocates leaves me pessimistic. If they had a ghost of a chance of giving me what I want, they wouldn't need to twist the English language.

November 29, 2009

Notes

1. "Cryonics." *Wikipedia.* "Drake Equation." *Wikipedia.*
2. Huemer, Michael. "What Is The Mind/Body Problem?" *University of Colorado*, 1992.

Why Pack for the Same Trip Twice?

Travelers often repeatedly visit the same family members, the same friends. Each visit normally requires two packing sessions: You pack the stuff you'll need, then repack the stuff you brought. Each leg takes time and energy, and possibly — depending on the airline — $25 to $50 per bag in out-of-pocket cost. Worse still, each packing session entails a risk of aggravating memory lapse. One time, you forget a belt; another, your toothpaste. Grrr.

There is a better way. Unless your family or friends live in very confined quarters, politely ask to permanently store one trip's worth of supplies at each destination. If your hosts appreciate you, they'll probably say yes. From then on, you can visit them without traditional packing. The out-of-pocket cost is modest. And in any case, if you have the means to travel in the First World, out-of-pocket costs should be secondary to your time, effort, and aggravation costs. Truth be told, you probably have several suitcases worth of clothes you rarely wear; why not pack them up and store them in several destinations you frequent? One fixed cost can save you years of marginal costs.

Sure, if *everyone* did this, it might cease to be good advice. You probably don't want to store twenty suitcases for your twenty closest friends — and your closest friends probably feel the same way. But so what? Hardly anyone follows my strategy now, and that's unlikely to change. And even if my idea caught on, triage is the obvious response. Store your stuff at the five places you visit most often, and reciprocate for your five most frequent guests.

Right now, I store a lot of stuff at my parents' house, and several useful items at Fabio Rojas' place. But I plan to take this a lot further. Next time I visit my parents, I'm leaving a week's stuff behind. I'll encourage them to do the same at my house. And when my kids have places of their own, I hope each will provide a few cubic feet for Grandpa Bryan.

Question: Why do so few people use my strategy? The awkwardness of asking? Hostility of the hosts' spouse? Or just plain old-fashioned status quo bias?

February 23, 2015

10 Things I Learned in
My First 10 Years of Parenting

My eldest sons just turned ten, which means I've been a father for ten years. Ergo, it's time to inventory the top things I've learned from my decade of experience. In no particular order:

1. Kids are a consumption good, and always have been.[1]

2. Have kids to create beloved companions, pay forward the gift of life, and see the world anew, not to get a person to mold or boss around.[2]

3. Discover things you and your kids enjoy doing together, and make plenty of time to actually do them.

4. You have little effect on your child's intelligence, success, or even character.[3] But you have a genuine effect on his appreciation of you — how he feels about and remembers you.

5. Your kid's preferences may differ from your childhood preferences, but it's still helpful to remember and try to be the kind of parent you wish you'd had.

6. Don't use discipline to turn your kid into a good person when he's an adult. It won't work. Use discipline to turn your

kid into a good roommate when he's a kid. It won't work miracles, but it's way better than nothing.[4]

7. Mild discipline, mechanically enforced, deters bad behavior far more effectively than harsh discipline, arbitrarily enforced. Idle threats, no matter how lurid, ("I'll sell you to the gypsies if you don't eat your dinner" "I'll turn this car to Disneyland right around") do not improve behavior at all.

8. Never lie to your children. Kids soon see through your deception, reputation matters, and in any case, lying is wrong.

9. Expressing anger at your children is counter-productive. It undermines your authority and gives wayward children hope of besting you.

10. Raise your children with kindness and respect. When they behave badly, calmly carry out promised punishments like Javert, then restart the game like Valjean.[5]

Bonus lesson: If your kids say you're embarrassing them, they're probably right. Don't argue, don't tease, just stop.

December 10, 2012

Notes

1. Caplan, Bryan. "Was Having Kids Ever a Paying Venture?" *EconLog*, October 16, 2009.
2. Caplan, Bryan. "The Weird Reason to Have More Kids." *EconLog*, December 2, 2010. Caplan, Bryan. "The Economics of the Gift of Life." *EconLog*, August 29, 2010.
3. Caplan, Bryan. *Selfish Reasons to Have More Kids.*

2011. Caplan, Bryan. "The Science of Success." *Econ-Log*, November 15, 2010.

4. Caplan, Bryan. "Discipline: Advice and Evidence." *EconLog*, August 20, 2010.

5. "Les Miserables — The First Attack." *YouTube*, May 29, 2011.

10 More Things I Learned in My First 10 Years of Parenting

fter I finished my last post, parenting life lessons kept coming to mind. Ten more:

1. You cannot be a bad spouse and a good parent.[1]

2. Do not let your kids ignore you. If your words call for a response, immediately make your question more and more blatant until you receive a response.

3. Do not give your kids a good reason to ignore you by being a repetitive windbag.

4. Do not change your parenting decisions in response to your kids' complaining, repeated requests, or other rent-seeking.[2] Caplan family motto: "Complaining gets you *nowhere* in this family."

5. If you lack the willpower to resist your kids' rent-seeking on an issue, magnanimously give them what they would have extracted from you under duress. You won't get your way, but at least you won't blatantly reinforce their bad behavior.[3]

6. At minimum, behavioral economics accurately describes children's behavior: myopia, the endowment effect, availability

bias, the works.

7. Other parents are pathological hazers. Ignore them. The average parent is probably less happy than the average non-parent, but being average is a *choice*.[4]

8. "To have kids" or "Not to have kids" are the fundamental lifestyle options. Once you have your first child, the marginal cost of another child is small. By the age of two, a pair of twins is often easier than a singleton.

9. T.V. is your friend — and if you think T.V. rots the brain, you aren't searching hard enough for good shows. *The Simpsons* is at least as good as Shakespeare.

10. Reduce the ambition of your family vacations until you have zero desire to scream at your kids or your spouse. The memory of one bad parental fight can easily overwrite a child's memory of an otherwise magical week.

Bonus lesson: "I'm your parent, not your friend" should mean "I'll treat you better than any friend ever will" — not "I'll treat you worse than any friend will ever dare."

To close on a sad note: Show zero tolerance for irresponsible driving, and don't worry about being "fair" when you confiscate car keys. Driving is the most dangerous activity young people in our society engage in, the accident rate is highly responsive to choice, and the real world often refuses to give a high-risk driver a second chance.[5]

December 11, 2012

Notes

1. Caplan, Bryan. "The Rotten Spouse Theorem." *EconLog*, October 17, 2011.
2. Henderson, David. "Rent Seeking." *EconLog.*
3. "Reinforcement." *Wikipedia.*
4. Caplan, Bryan. "Married with 19 Kids = Single and Childless." *EconLog*, April 14, 2008. Caplan, Bryan. "An Economist's Guide to Happier Parenting." *EconLog*, June 25, 2006.
5. Caplan, Bryan. "Modernity as a Children's Paradise." *EconLog*, August 7, 2009.

An Economist's Guide
to Happier Parenting

Happiness research hits a lot of nerves, but the finding that kids don't make people happier may be the unkindest cut of all. As a proponent of having more kids, I could make methodological objections, but the truth is, I do notice a lot of people who don't seem to enjoy being parents.[1] My view, however, is that to a fair degree, these parents just *aren't doing it right*! Fortunately, basic economics is here to lend a helping hand.

My main observation about parental unhappiness is this: The last 10% of parenting hours causes half of all the parental unhappiness. First two hours with your kids: a joy. Second two hours: pretty good. Hours 5-8: Tolerable. Hours nine and ten: Pain. Remaining hours: Anguish. There are few better illustrations of the law of diminishing marginal utility.

Once you see this clearly, there are some obvious solutions:

1. Don't bite off more than you can chew. Don't plan three activities every Saturday, and wind up exploding at your kids' behavior in the middle of the third. It's far better for them and

you to do one thing together that you can all enjoy, then let them watch t.v. Seriously.

2. If you can afford a nanny, get a nanny. If you can't afford a nanny yet, consider waiting to have kids until you can. If you're the typical person who isn't sure if he or she wants kids, you're well-educated and have good income potential. So if you can't afford a nanny yet, you'll be able to soon enough.

3.   Don't let American prejudice against live-in nannies influence you: Live-in nannies mean you can sleep in, stay out, and get a break when you need one. Your best bet is to get a mature woman to bond with your kids when they're infants, and keep her happy. A little respect goes a long way.

4.   Read Judith Harris' *The Nurture Assumption.*[2] Don't worry about "molding" your child for life; you couldn't do it if you tried. Realize, instead, that the purpose of discipline is:

a. To keep your kid in one piece.

b. To make your life easier — you count too!

c. To force your kid to sacrifice *very* short-run gains (playing ten more minutes) for short-run gains (not being cranky later today)

Thus, I am adamant about naps. Partly this is because little kids get cranky without their naps, but refuse to accept the fact. But mostly it's because *I'll* be cranky if I don't get a nap, and I can't nap if they don't.

If you can't mold your child, what's the point? As Harris observes, that's a lot like asking "If you can't mold your wife, what's the point?" *The point is to enjoy your time together.* If you spend most of your time trying to make your kid be something he's not, no wonder you're not enjoying yourself — and don't expect your kid to be grateful for your efforts.

How would you like it if someone you depended on kept

trying to change you? It's even more foolish to try to change a kid, because he's likely to change in the desired direction all on his own, in time. In the end, your kid will probably be a lot like you.

June 25, 2006

Notes

1. Gilbert, Daniel. "Stumbling on Happiness." *Random House.* Caplan, Bryan. "Selfish Reasons to Have More Kids." *EconLog*, January 19, 2005.
2. Harris, Judith. *The Nurture Assumption: Why Children Turn Out the Way They Do*, 2009.

Part III

Professor Homeschool

How I Love Education

When I write about education, I suspect I come off as a philistine. You might even boil my position down to: "Students are bored, and aren't acquiring job skills, so their education is a waste of time and money." But what about learning for its own sake? Why do I seem so closed to the possibility that education is a *merit good* that human beings ought to consume to uplift their souls?[1]

This question is awkward for me because, unlike many economists and libertarians, I actually believe in merit goods. For example, I believe that opera — especially 19th-century German opera — is the objective pinnacle of musical a-chievement. Given my stance, it's also natural to see great intrinsic value in the study of philosophy, history, literature, and the like. Truth be told, "impractical" education is central to my whole sense of identity. How can I live with myself when I ridicule the magic of education?[2]

My answer: I love education *too much* to respect the mediocre substitutes that schools actually offer. How do these substitutes fall short of my ideals?

1. Education, like opera, is only a merit good *when it's done right*. Real-world opera, happily, usually *is* done right. Real-world education, in contrast, is a travesty. Most educators are boring. They fail to bring the liveliest of subjects to life. They focus on irrelevant details and hollow technique. And in the social sciences and humanities, many of the "great ideas" and "great thinkers" aren't just wrong, but stupidly wrong.

Take Marxism. As far as I'm concerned, it's no more a merit good than creation science.[3] Grasping the thoughts of economically illiterate 19th-century hate-mongers is not a crucial ingredient of a life well-lived.

2. Education, like opera, is only a merit good *when experienced by minds capable of seriously appreciating it.* Exposing bright, artistic minds to opera is great. Pushing opera on apathetic NASCAR fans is a waste of time — and can easily ruin the experience for genuine opera aficionados. The same goes for philosophy, history, literature, and the like. Exposing bright, logical minds to philosophy is great. Pushing philosophy on apathetic undergraduates is a waste of time at best.

Sure, there's some uncertainty about who's really open to great ideas. But there's far less uncertainty than educators like to tell themselves. Convincing a random student that "epistemology is fascinating" is virtually impossible. In the typical UC Berkeley class for philosophy *majors,* I rarely found more than two or three students who cared enough about the subject to study it on their own initiative.

Can't education be improved? Yes, but major reform is unlikely. As long as professors make money while ruining great subjects, and the labor market rewards students for feigning interest, the charade will go on.[4]

My standards may seem unreasonably high. But they're

typically realized in, for example, the Institute for Humane Studies' summer seminars.[5] A few professors who love teaching and have something they're burning to say deliver two or three lectures a piece. A few dozen self-selected students from around the world show up and happily participate. The students receive no academic credit, just a week of learning, sharing, and debating mind-blowing ideas.

I love these summer seminars. They're beautiful. They're a merit good. And they bear almost no resemblance to the official coursework students have to endure to get a diploma.

July 18, 2012

Notes

1. "Merit Good." *Wikipedia.*
2. Caplan, Bryan. "The Magic of Education." *EconLog*, November 28, 2011.
3. "Creation Science." *Wikipedia.*
4. Caplan, Bryan. "Stably Wasteful: Why New Tech Won't Gut Higher Education." *EconLog*, October 24, 2011.
5. "Events and Programs." *Institute for Humane Studies.*

Good Students Rule

Most professors *like* good students, but I idolize them. For most professors, good students are a joy in the classroom, but a chore outside of the classroom. For me, good students are a joy through and through. I like talking with them, lunching with them, and even gaming with them.[1]

Good students have four key traits.

First, good students genuinely want to learn. They don't study material merely because they see it on the syllabus or expect it on the test.

Second, good students fight the natural human tendency to forget material right after the final exam. Unlike most students, they consciously choose to try to remember what they learn.

Third, good students strive for what educational psychologists call Transfer of Learning.[2] They earnestly try to apply what they've learned *outside* the classroom.

Fourth, and perhaps most importantly, good students put Truth first. They aren't afraid to entertain and embrace socially unacceptable ideas.

How can one become a good student? While decent IQ is important, being a good student is, to a large extent, a choice. Admit that there are important intellectual questions. Resist your impulsive answers.[3] Don't worry about what people in your society are supposed to think. Calmly listen to the arguments of people who have reflected on the important intellectual questions longer than you have. Cross-examine the arguments. Apply your lessons to concrete cases. Do all this, and you're well on your way to being a good student.

What's so great about good students? Selfishly speaking, they're fun to be around. I've spent decades searching for answers. It's great to share what I've found with eager minds in search of shortcuts. Entertainment value aside, though, good students make the world a better place. Imagine political debates — or public policy! — if every voter were a good student.

If I admire good students so much, how can I make *The Case Against Education*?[4] Because, as I've explained before, good students deserve something radically different from the status quo.[5] People who care about learning should be surrounded by other students who feel the same way. In actual education systems, however, most students just grub credentials to signal for the labor market. Bad students sharply outnumber good students — even in grad school. Most teachers react as you'd expect: By catering to the vast majority of anti-intellectual careerists in their classrooms. Better teachers try to raise the bar, but giving good students a passable experience is an uphill battle when 90% of the class doesn't even want to be there.

Still, as always, we should focus on the positive. Today is the first day of a new academic year. I'll soon meet my latest wave of good students. They're going to be awesome. All the problems with the status quo notwithstanding, another great pedagogical journey is about to begin.

August 26, 2013

Notes

1. Caplan, Bryan. "Gaming on EconLog: A History of Nerddom." *EconLog*, August 14, 2013.
2. Caplan, Bryan. "Low Transfer of Learning: The Glass is Half Full." *EconLog*, Augsut 21, 2012.
3. Caplan, Bryan. "Eureka! Economic Illiteracy as Mental Substitution." *EconLog*, January 10, 2012.
4. Caplan, Bryan. "The Magic of Education." *EconLog*, November 28, 2011.
5. Caplan, Bryan. "How I Love Education." *EconLog*, July 18, 2012.

Separating Twins
as Economic Illiteracy

S chools usually try to put twins in different classes. In part, it's for the convenience of the teacher — identical twins can be hard to tell apart. But the main rationale is that if you separate twins, they will *make more new friends*. Isn't that great?

If you've had a week of intro economics, I hope your answer is "No." Consider: What would you do if aliens abducted all of your friends? In all likelihood, you'd wind up making a bunch of new friends, right? But it would be absurd to claim that the aliens had done you a favor. Before the body snatchers came along, you'd didn't *need* those new friends, because you were happy with the ones you already had. To argue otherwise is just make-work bias.[1]

The same logic applies to splitting up twins. Sure, if you separate twins, they'll make more friends. But that hardly means you're doing them a favor. The reason why twins put less effort into making new friends is that they've already got a better friend than most of us will ever have. For twins, the marginal benefit of trying to make new friends is unusually small — and cliquishness is their optimal response.

You could argue, admittedly, that kids underestimate the benefit of making new friends. But what reason is there is to believe that this is true? And in any case, that's no reason to specifically target twins. If you really believed that kids had an "anti-new-friends bias", you'd ask *all* parents to name their kids' best friends, and make a effort to separate as many children as possible from the kids they like the most. "You'll thank me later," right?

A decade or two ago, pundits often said that the Japanese economy was doing well because all their factories were destroyed during World War II. As a result, the story went, the Japanese built shiny new factories from scratch, and the victors with their musty old plants just couldn't compete. The standard economists' response to this nonsense: "If that's true, all we need to do to catch up to the Japanese is just bomb our own factories!"

Folks who want to separate twins are making the same mistake. We always have the option of "destroying in order to rebuild." But it's usually a bad idea — especially if you're destroying over the objection of the people you're trying to help.

So what should we do with twins? Simple: Ask them what *they* want to do. If they want to stay together, keep them together. If they want to separate and develop their individuality, split them up. And if you're really sure that "Stay together" is the wrong answer, why not try to convince us with a little self-experimentation?[2] Cut the time you spend with your best friend in half, and tell us how you like it…

December 22, 2008

Notes

1. Caplan, Bryan. "The 4 Boneheaded Biases of Stupid Voters." *Reason*, October, 2007.
2. Cowen, Tyler. "Self-Experimentation." *Marginal Revolution*, February 18, 2007.

The Iron Laws of Pedagogy

E veryone who's ever been a student can vouch for what
I call the Iron Laws of Pedagogy:

First Iron Law: *Students learn only a small fraction
of what they're taught.*

Second Iron Law: *Students remember only a small fraction of
what they learn.*

Third Iron Law: *Most of the lessons students remember lack
practical applications.*

Research on Transfer of Learning strongly confirms a
fourth, less obvious conclusion:[1]

Fourth Iron Law: *Even when students remember something
with practical applications, they still usually fail to apply what
they know... unless you explicitly tell them to do so.*

If you're tempted to yawn at these truisms, reread the
Fourth Iron Law. Anyone who jumps through the hoops of
formal education witnesses its multiplicative inadequacies. Yet
when former students argue about education policy, most fail
to apply their first-hand knowledge — precisely as the Fourth
Law predicts! What do they do instead? Give in to wishful

thinking and Social Desirability Bias — and hail education as the key to the universe.[2]

October 18, 2013

Notes

1. Caplan, Bryan. "Low Transfer of Learning: The Glass is Half Full." *EconLog*, August 21, 2012.
2. Caplan, Bryan. "The Public Goods Model vs. Social Desirability Bias: A Case of Observational Equivalence." *EconLog*, September 4, 2012.

The Economics and Philosophy of Pity Grades

M ore students than I care to remember have argued with me about their grades. But there is one argument that I always dismiss out of hand: "You should raise my grade because I NEED a higher grade!" I don't do pity grading.

You could argue against pity grading on reputational grounds. If employers, other schools, and parents knew that pity grading went on, it would make all grades less informative. Does this applicant have an A because he was an A student, or had a soft-hearted teacher? Did my son maintain the B average I demand through hard work, or by telling the teacher "My dad will kick me out of the house unless you give me an A-"?

I could make this argument, but it would be dishonest. The *real* reason I refuse to pity grade is not that it will degrade the informational value of grades. If raising a student's grade would double his lifetime income, and I knew with absolute certainty that no one would ever find out, I still wouldn't do it.

So why not bend the rules? My objection to doing so is

that students should get the grade they *earned*. And this has nothing to do with how much higher grades would benefit them. Students who demonstrate their knowledge of the material deserve high grades, and students who demonstrate their lack of knowledge deserve low grades, and that's all there is to it. In short, morally correct grading is about merit, not need.

What if some students had more opportunities than others? It makes no difference. A student who does not know labor economics fails my class, even if the reason he does not know it is because he had to work two jobs to support his grandma. Should we take Olympic gold medals away from the children of parents who supported their dream from the cradle on? I think not.

Maybe I deeply misread them, but I suspect that even most left-wing professors grade as meritocratically as I do. They may give extra help to students who come to office hours, but if a student spends two hours in your office every week and still fails the exam, you can't let him slide.

To me, this reveals a basic inconsistency in egalitarian philosophy. If you assign grades based on merit, and merit depends on performance unadjusted for opportunity, then why shouldn't the same principle hold for income and wealth? Just because you feel sorry for someone, why does that entitle them to a share of the riches of the more successful? And if you do not adjust for unequal opportunities when you grade, why should you adjust for unequal opportunities when you contemplate redistribution?

You could say that money affects people's lives more than grades, but I beg to differ. The empirical evidence cuts the other way.[1] Job satisfaction — which probably depends heavily on having the education and grades to open up the doors you want to walk through — matters a lot more for happiness than dollars of income. So if you really wanted to even out the ultimate inequality of life, you'd redistribute grades before money.

Yes, all this sounds harsh. I've never claimed to be a Bleeding-Heart Libertarian.[2] What I will admit is that I often *admire* the student who comes in second despite his disadvantages more than the student who comes in first. But I see no inconsistency. Prizes are the wages of merit; admiration is the wage of virtue.

August 17, 2005

Notes

1. Caplan, Bryan. "Money and Happiness: Double-Check With the GSS." *EconLog*, August 9, 2005.
2. Caplan, Bryan. "Let Them Get Roommates." *EconLog*, March 25, 2005.

How I Teach When I Really
Want My Students to Learn

A month ago, my eleven-year-old sons still didn't know how to tie their shoes. I volunteered to teach them. As a professional educator, I was tempted to teach shoe-tying the same way I teach econ: with a scintillating lecture. Since I *really* wanted my sons to learn how to tie their shoes, however, I did no such thing. Instead, I followed these six steps.

Step 1: Make the task easier. They were struggling to tie their shoes on their feet. So I had them place their shoes on the table and learn to tie them there. I also ordered easy-to-grip flat shoelaces to replace the round laces that came with the shoes.

Step 2: Break shoe-tying into a dozen sequential actions: cross the laces, pull the laces tight, form left and right rabbit ears, etc.

Step 3: Show them how to do the first action. Then place my hands over their hands while they do the first action. Then have them do it on their own, correcting any deviations from best practice. Repeat. Repeat. Repeat.

Step 4: Practice only ten minutes per day regardless of success to avoid frustration.

Step 5: Once they reach near-mastery on the first action, tack on the second action and go back to Step 3. Keep tacking on actions until they master the whole sequence.

Step 6: Now, practice the same sequence with shoes on the feet. Repeat to mastery.

I almost — but not quite — went full behaviorist.[1] 95% of the lesson was hands-on. Instead of lecturing, I recited shoe-tying catechisms: "Make the rabbit ears. Hand one-third up the lace. Make the rabbit ears. One-third. Not half. Make the rabbit ears." I never challenged my sons to ponder the deep nature of shoe-tying; I only wanted to impart the practical skill. When they made mistakes, I asked them to recite the catechism, correcting any deviations as they happened.

My lessons were fully effective. Before long, my sons were experts — and so they will remain for their whole lives. Which led to an awkward realization: My technique for teaching shoe-tying is much more effective than my technique for teaching economics. In my experience, only 5-10% of my students master the material by the final exam. And even my best students tend to quickly forget most of what they learned.[2]

I'm tempted to lament the Iron Laws of Pedagogy.[3] But my shoe-tying experience tells me that's a cop-out. I *know* how to make my students learn more. If filling my students with life-long knowledge were my top priority, I'd replace my thoughtful lectures with catechisms. I'd make the students chant aloud with me. I'd break every lesson into baby steps, and drive the students to master them one by one. How? I'd randomly and mercilessly put students on the spot, pressing them to apply the lesson aloud — and correct the slightest misstep. We'd meet seven days a week for half an hour, endlessly recapping what we've learned. Sure, I'd cover far less ground. Yet after a semester, my students would know the basics for a lifetime.

Why don't I do this? While I could say, "The best way to teach shoe-tying is radically different from the best way to teach economics," that's an excuse. The truth: I don't teach econ the same way I teaching shoe-tying because I'd hate it, and my students would hate me.

I don't wish to be a mere drill sergeant who turns raw recruits into competent economists. I want to be an artist who turns economics into a magical journey. I want to challenge my best students, not teach to the lowest common denominator.[4] And my students, for their part, want to sit back and relax. They don't want me to randomly shine the classroom spotlight on them, ask questions, demand answers, and make them feel stupid over and over until they know what they're talking about. One midterm, one final: That's enough stress for a semester.

Now that you've heard my pedagogical confession, you might expect me to turn over a new leaf. I probably won't. I love old-fashioned teaching too much to walk away. And what's the point of adopting more effective teaching techniques if students refuse to take my classes?

July 3, 2014

Notes

1. "Behaviorism." *Wikipedia.*

2. Caplan, Bryan. "The Career Consequences of Failing Versus Forgetting." *EconLog*, February 9, 2012.
3. Caplan, Bryan. "The Iron Laws of Pedagogy." *EconLog*, October 18, 2013.
4. Caplan, Bryan. "Good Students Rule." *EconLog*, August 26, 2013.

Teaching Teaching

Over the last three years, my older sons have gone from near-zero knowledge of Spanish to fluency. Given my open disdain for foreign language education, what's the backstory?[1]

I started them in 9th grade because almost all good colleges impose an admission requirement of 3-4 years of foreign language instruction. From the outset, my boys planned to demonstrate their competence on the Spanish Language AP test. Going through the motions would not suffice; we knew my sons actually had to learn a lot of Spanish. After a few sour months, fortunately, my sons started to like their new subject. Then they became obsessed... in a good way. Now they've taken college classes for natives in Spain and Guatemala, written a publishable paper on Mexican history using primary sources, and mostly speak Spanish to each other.[2]

Since our emergency homeschool contains these two fluent Spanish-speakers, I thought it might be fruitful for my older sons to teach Spanish to their younger siblings.[3] After all, the younger ones are going to need a foreign language for college one day, too.

The catch: When Spanish instruction began last week, I realized that my older sons knew Spanish, but not how to teach. As a result, I'm teaching teaching while they're teaching Spanish. Since I've been teaching professionally for about 25 years, its principles are second nature to me. Yet if you're now teaching for the first time in your life, they're non-obvious. Indeed, in my experience, over half of working teachers fail to internalize them. As Morpheus admonishes in *The Matrix*, "Neo, sooner or later you're going to realize, just as I did, that there's a difference between knowing the path and walking the path."

Principles of Effective Teaching

1. Take the difficulty level you naturally want to use. *Now divide it by 10.* Remember: The material is only obvious to you because you are the teacher. It is non-obvious to your students because they are the students.

2. If you're teaching at MIT or Caltech, you are now at the right difficulty level. If you're anywhere else, *divide by 10 again.* Remember: Even smart people are, at first, terrible at almost everything.

3. Don't expects students to "figure things out for themselves." Start with model problems, then work through them at a snail's pace.

4. Once you have shown students clear model problems, assign a bunch of slightly different problems. Tell them to get to work. Mush!

5. If your students do less than 75% of their problems correctly, your problems are still too hard. Walk them through problems so easy you can't even imagine their inability to do them. This will improve their knowledge and your imagina-

tion.

6. If your students do 75-94% of their problems correctly, give them more practice. Drill, drill, drill.

7. If your students do 95%+ of their problems correctly, they are ready to advance. Even then, remember that they are likely to forget unless you periodically give them refresher work (except for highly sequential subjects).[4]

8. Never confuse logic with psycho-logic — and remember that psycho-logic is much more important for pedagogy. What does that mean? Don't expect students to grasp that A–>B simply because A–>B. Your job is to make truisms *seem* obvious to ignorant minds. Vary your examples. Mix it up. Switch around. Use repetition. Use repetition. Use repetition.

9. Look at your students' faces. If they are bored, *be more fun*. Tell jokes. Mock yourself. Clown around. Playfully exaggerate all emotions. Throw your pride aside; a teacher is an entertainer or he is a failure.

10. Look at your students' faces. If they are frustrated, be more patient. Never add negative emotion on top of negative emotion. If a student is upset, be a model of mild-mannered stoicism. Without fail. Without fail. Without fail.

11. Look at your students' faces. If they feel like their efforts are pointless, sell them your subject. Tell them what learning your subject will do for them, even if the only honest answer is, "You need this for graduation."

12. Look at your students' faces. If they don't trust you, *earn their trust*. Don't merely avoid deception; *be frank*. Don't sugarcoat the world, even for little kids. Unless the ugly truth will give them nightmares or get you fired, share it with equanimity.

13. Look at your students' faces. If you can't read their

emotions, ask them questions. Press them. Find out what they already know. Find out what confuses them. Find out whether they are happy or sad or think you're crazy. Accept their answers beatifically and adjust your pedagogy to fit the students you actually have.

14. Maintain discipline. If you have a schedule, stick to it. If you announce a punishment, stick to it. If you promise a break, stick to it. Education is *for* the students, but it is not a democracy. Listen carefully to what your students say, but only reform from a position of strength. Don't be generous; be magnanimous! If you think this contradicts Principle #9, know that you are wrong. Act like a jester — but rule like a king.

15. All of these principles are optimized for one-on-one teaching. If you're teaching more students, you have to strike a balance. You will always shortchange someone. Sorry, that's a classroom — another point in favor of homeschooling. [5]

April 2, 2020

Notes

1. Caplan, Bryan. "The Degree and Origin of Foreign Language Competence." *EconLog*, August 11, 2012.
2. Caplan, Bryan. "Reflections from Spain." *EconLog*, July 17, 2019. Caplan, Bryan. "Reflections on Guatemala." *EconLog*, March 2, 2020.
3. Caplan, Bryan. "Emergency Homeschooling: A How-To Guide." *EconLog*, March 23, 2020.

4. Caplan, Bryan. "Forgetting: The Basic Facts." *EconLog*, January 21, 2016.
5. Caplan, Bryan. "Why I'm Homeschooling." *EconLog*, September 22, 2015.

Why I'm Homeschooling

I'm homeschooling my elder sons for middle school.[1] On the surface, this makes sense: Homeschooling has been in the libertarian penumbra for decades.[2] If you know my books, however, you should be puzzled.

1. In *Selfish Reasons to Have More Kids*, I argue that the power of nurture is vastly overrated.[3] Genetics, not upbringing, explains almost all of the observed similarity between parent and child. It's not reasonable, then, for me to expect my efforts to durably boost my kids' IQs, educational success, income, or even their political views.

2. In *The Case Against Education*, I argue that signaling, not human capital, explains most of the effect of education on earnings.[4] Without an established school's seal of approval, learning has little selfish payoff. So even if the Caplan Family School manages to build stellar cognitive skills, the Real World won't reward them.

Of course, it would be deeply out of character for me to homeschool without replies to both objections. Here they are:

1. While the power of nurture to change kids' *adult outcomes* is indeed vastly overrated, it is well within my power to give my sons a better *childhood*. My kids prefer a challenging academic curriculum. I can give them that. My kids hate music, dance, art, and group projects. I can spare them these indignities. My kids don't want to wake up at 5:45 AM every morning. In the Caplan Family School, we start at a civilized hour. Homeschooling gives my sons plenty of time for math, reading, and history, but leaves them ample free time for hobbies and travel.[5]

More speculative: I suspect — though I'm far from sure — that the Caplan Family School is such an exceptional experience that ordinary twin and adoption evidence isn't relevant.[6] For example, my sons are plausibly the only 12-year-olds in the nation taking a college class in labor economics.[7] Perhaps it really will forever rock their worlds. More obviously, their peer group now includes Robin Hanson, Alex Tabarrok, Tyler Cowen, Garett Jones, and Nathaniel Bechhofer. That's plausibly four standard deviations above whatever peer group they'd have in a conventional middle school.

2. While education is mostly signaling, there are cracks in the system. As far as I can tell, the Real World pays zero attention to what students do in middle school. The Caplan Family School won't keep my kids out of good high schools; they can re-enter Fairfax County Public School in 9th grade. It won't keep my kids out of good colleges; colleges don't know what applicants did in middle school. And it won't keep my kids from getting good jobs; there probably isn't an employer in the country who asks how applicants did in 7th grade. So while homeschooling feels risky for high school, our next two years look like clear sailing.

If my reasoning sounds familiar, it should. I'm a strategic non-conformist.[8] When I can bend stupid rules with impunity, I bend them.

September 22, 2015

Notes

1. Caplan, Bryan. "Caplan Family School Attendance Contract." *EconLog*, September 9, 2015.
2. Caplan, Bryan. "Libertarian Penumbra." *EconLog*, February 21, 2011.
3. Caplan, Bryan. *Selfish Reasons to Have More Kids*, 2011.
4. Caplan, Bryan. "The Case Against Education: What's Taking So Long." *EconLog*, March 6, 2015.
5. "Capla-Con." *Facebook*. Caplan, Bryan. "The Economics and Philosophy of the Cruise Ship." *EconLog*, July 21, 2005.
6. Caplan, Bryan. "Are Twin Studies 'Pretty Much Useless'?" *EconLog*, August 26, 2011.
7. Caplan, Bryan. "Econ 321: Labor Economics." *George Mason University*.
8. Caplan, Bryan. "A Non-Conformist's Guide to Success in a Conformist World." *EconLog*, July 28, 2014.

The World's Worst Argument
Against Homeschooling

I've heard many arguments against homeschooling.[1] Here's the worst:

"Bryan, you've got to send your kids back to public high school."

"Why?"

"Well, you've got to understand that high school is miserable."

"I remember it well. How is that an argument *for* high school?"

"Because it prepares you for the misery of life. Having a job is just like being in high school. Without that preparation, you'll never make it in the real world."

The obvious objection: Suppose your kid is incredibly happy in high school. *Everyone*'s nice and encouraging. He's learning piles of material. Day after day, he comes home and says, "High school is a dream come true." What kind of a parent would react not with elation, but alarm? As in: "Eek! My kid may be excelling academically, but he's totally not being prepared for the harshness of adult life. I've got to immediately move him to a school where he's unhappy... for his own good!" None I've ever encountered.

Sure, parents occasionally sentence their kids to military school, but they do so because the kid is behaving badly *now*, not because they fear that their studious, well-mannered kids will grow up to be snowflakes.

So what's the *best* argument against homeschooling? Conformity signaling, of course.[2]

April 27, 2017

Notes

1. Caplan, Bryan. "Why I'm Homeschooling." *EconLog*, September 22, 2015.
2. Caplan, Bryan. "Signaling Versus Educational Innovation." *EconLog*, April 16, 2012.

Unschooling + Math

One popular variant on homeschooling is called "unschooling." The practice varies, as practices always do. The essence, however, is that the student does what he wants. He studies what he wants. He studies for as long as he wants. If he asks you to teach him something, you teach him. Yet if he decides to play videogames all day, the principled unschooling response is: "Let him."

Almost every parent is horrified by the idea of unschooling. Even most homeschoolers shake their heads. Advocates insist, however, that unschooling works. Psychologist Peter Gray defends the merits of unschooling with great vigor and eloquence.[1] According to unschoolers, the human child is naturally curious. Given freedom, he won't just learn basic skills; he'll ultimately find a calling.

On the surface, unschooling sounds like Social Desirability Bias run amok: "Oh yes, every child *loves* to learn, it's just society that fails them!"[2] And as a mortal enemy of Social Desirability Bias, my instinct is to dismiss unschooling out of hand.[3]

One thing I loathe more than Social Desirability Bias, however, is refusing to calm down and look at the facts. Fact: I've personally met and conversed with dozens of adults who were unschooled. Overall, they appear at least as well-educated as typical graduates from the public school system. Indeed, as Gray would predict, unschoolers are especially likely to turn their passions into careers. Admittedly, some come across as flaky, but then again so do a lot young people.

When you look closely, unschoolers have only one obvious problem: *They're weak in math!*

In my experience, even unschoolers with stellar IQs tend to be weak in algebra. Algebra, I say! And their knowledge of more advanced mathematics is sparser still.

Staunch unschoolers will reply: So what? Who needs algebra? The honest answer, though, is: Anyone who wants to pursue a vast range of high-status occupations. STEM requires math. CS requires math. Social science requires math. Even sophisticated lawyers — the kind that discuss investments' Net Present Values — require math.

Won't kids who would greatly benefit from math choose to learn math given the freedom to do so? The answer, I fear, is: rarely. For two reasons:

First, math is extremely unfun for almost everyone. Only a handful of nerds sincerely finds the subject engaging. I'm a big nerd, and I've done piles of math, yet I've never really liked it.

Second, math is highly cumulative. Each major stage of math builds on the foundation of the previous stages. If you reach adulthood and *then* decide to learn math to pursue a newly-discovered ambition, I wish you good luck, because you'll need it.

What's the best response? Mainstream critics of unschooling will obviously use this criticism to dismiss the entire approach.

And staunch unschoolers will no doubt stick to their guns. I, however, propose a keyhole solution.[4] I call it: Unschooling + Math.

What does Unschooling + Math mean? Simple: Impose a single parental mandate on unschooled children. Every day, like it or not, you have to do 1-2 hours of math. No matter how boring you find the subject, you're too young to decide that you don't want to pursue a career that requires math. And if you postpone the study of math for long, it will be too late to start later on.

While most people *don't* wind up using much math on the job, ignorance of basic math is still a severe handicap in life.[5] And when smart kids don't know advanced math, they forfeit about half of all high-status career opportunities.

We should have a strong presumption against paternalism — even the literal paternalism of a parent for his own child.[6] "Maybe the kid is right and the parent is wrong" is a deeply underrated thought. The value of math, however, is great enough to overcome this presumption. To be clear, I *don't* mean that the government should force homeschoolers to teach math. What I mean, rather, is that homeschoolers should require their kids to learn math. Guilt-free.

October 27, 2020

Notes

1. Caplan, Bryan. "Play and Exit." *EconLog,* November 5, 2013.

2. Caplan, Bryan. "Social Desirability Bias: How Psych Can Salvage Econo-Cynicism." *EconLog*, April 21, 2014.

3. Caplan, Bryan. "The Freedom to Do What *Sounds Wrong*." *EconLog*, October 14, 2020.

4. Caplan, Bryan. "Keyhole Surgery with *The Undercover Economist*." *EconLog*, November 4, 2005.

5. Caplan, Bryan. "Does High School Algebra Pass a Cost-Benefit Test?" *EeconLog*, October 17, 2012.

6. Caplan, Bryan. "*Escaping Paternalism* Book Club Round-Up." *EconLog*, September 10, 2010.

Real Subjects Have No Arbiter

When you challenge the morality of the status quo, people usually leap to its defense. After a few rounds of argument, though, defenders of the status quo often retreat to meta-ethics. Maybe immigration restrictions do seem wrong.[1] But how are we to decide? Who precisely is the arbiter of right and wrong?

Faced with this question, I've long given the same answer: *No one* is the "arbiter" of right and wrong. Individuals just have to consider the moral issue and form their best judgment. That hardly makes morality subjective.[2] There's no arbiter of scientific or historical truth, either.

I now realize that my answer could have been stronger all along. Yes, there's no arbiter of scientific truth, of historical truth, of moral truth. But what truths — if any — *do* have an arbiter? When, if ever, is there a Decider of truth?

There is a simple answer: arbiters do indeed exist — but only for purely social truths.[3] If your question is, "Are Jack and Mary married?," an arbiter might exist. After all, to be married is nothing more than to be *considered* married by a society. If the people in a society accept the Grand Poobah as the arbiter of marriage, then *whatever he decides* about two people's marital status is their true martial status.

Similarly: If the people of the United States accept the Supreme Court as the arbiter of constitutionality, then it *is* the arbiter. If people play a game where the rules say the Game Master is always right, then the Game Master is the arbiter of that game. Etc.

What do all these arbiters have in common? Simple: Their subjects are all make-believe to begin with! That's why one person's judgment can be decisive: One version of "let's pretend" is "let's pretend that whatever X says, is true." Fake subjects can have arbiters because there are no underlying facts to get in the way.

The converse is also true: If a subject has an arbiter, that subject is fake. The fact that one person's say-so *decides* an issue reveals the make-believe nature of the issue. Picture how you'd react if someone claimed to be the Arbiter of Math. Impossible, right? But why? Because math is a real subject with real answers that are right or wrong no matter what anyone thinks.

When people ask, "Who's the arbiter of morality?," the correct answer is indeed "No one." But this answer, though correct, it is woefully incomplete. The critic's insinuation — morality is subjective because it lacks an arbiter — is the opposite of the truth. If morality had an arbiter, *that* would be a conclusive sign of its subjectivity. The fact that morality lacks an arbiter is one sign — though hardly a conclusive one — that morality, like science, history, and math — has answers that no one's mere say-so can undo.

June 25, 2012

Notes

1. Caplan, Bryan. "Tell Me the Difference Between Jim Crow and Immigration Restrictions." *EconLog*, March 7, 2012.
2. Huemer, Michael. "Moral Objectivism" *University of Colorado.*
3. Searle, John. *The Construction of Social Reality*, 1997.

Seven Guidelines for Writing Worthy Works of Non-Fiction

I try to write the kind of books I'd like to read, and I try to read the kind of books I'd like to write. This isn't as narcissistic as it sounds. I'd *like* to write like Tolstoy or Alan Moore or Steve Landsburg, but I have to settle for being me.

As far as fiction goes, I don't have enough experience to pontificate.[1] But I propose the following guidelines for writing worthy works of non-fiction:

1. Pick an important topic. If someone asks you, "What are the five most important areas to think about?," and you're writing about something that isn't on your own list, you should be disturbed. How do you know if a topic is important? My test: If everyone on earth read your book and believed it, would it make the world a better place? (Note: That's a test of importance, not truth!)

2. Learn a lot about your topic. Start with standard academic literatures, but don't stop there. Cast a wider net. See if other disciplines study your topic under a different label. See what

134

smart people throughout history thought about your topic. See what non-academics think too, even if they seem like idiots.

3. Keep telling yourself: "Once I perfect the organization of my book, it will practically write itself." If you're deviating from your own plan, either stop or change your plan. Related hypothesis: The main cause of non-fiction writer's block is lack of a clear chapter structure.

4. Never preach to the choir. It's impossible to be convincing to everyone. But if you haven't made a persuasive case to the reader who doesn't initially agree with you, start over. Remember: You're writing a book, not a diary.

5. When in doubt, write like Hemingway. If you can delete a word without changing the meaning of a sentence, do so.

6. Treat specific intellectual opponents with respect, in print and otherwise, even if they don't reciprocate. But feel free to ridicule ridiculous ideas.

7. Don't keep your cards close to your chest. Share your sincere probabilities with your readers. Don't just tell them what you can "prove." Tell them anything interesting that you're willing to bet on — and at what odds.

October 21, 2009

Notes

1. Caplan, Bryan. "Amore Infernale." *bcaplan.com*, 2007.

Part IV

How to Dale Carnegie

If the Angry Could Hear
What the Calm Do Not Say

Dear Angry Person,
   I can tell that you're angry at me again. I think I understand your complaint, though I have trouble understanding why this specific issue is upsetting you on this specific day. But based on past experience, asking for clarification will only make you angrier, without helping me avoid your future anger. As usual, then, I plan to appease you.[1]

   But in the silence of my mind, I've got a question for you. In all the years we've known each other, how many times have I expressed anger at you? By my count, the answer is... *zero*. Question: Do you think that's because your behavior is above reproach? Do you imagine I'm entirely satisfied with the way you've treated me? Well, I'm not. Your emotional abuse aside, you've failed to meet my expectations more than once.

   So why haven't I ever raised my voice at you? Indeed, why do I normally act as if everything you do is unobjectionable? Seven main reasons.

   1. Nobody's perfect. I take a moderate amount of bad

behavior for granted, and count myself lucky it's not worse.

2. Assessing behavior is surprisingly ambiguous. Real life is not a math exam. While bad behavior plainly exists, even decent people frequently see the world differently — an insight that inspired game theorists to develop the notion of trembling-hands equilibria.[2] In such an environment, interpreting people's actions charitably is advisable — especially people with a long, admirable track record.

3. While getting angry often changes behavior for the better, getting angry also often changes behavior for the worse. Net effect? Unclear.[3]

4. Getting angry is far from the *only* way to change behavior for the better. So in the subset of situations where anger is an effective motivator, you still have to ask: Does it motivate *better* than these alternatives? The answer, once again, is unclear.

5. Even when anger is the best short-run strategy, it damages long-run relationships. And I value these long-run relationships more than I value winning any specific dispute.

6. Getting angry clouds your thinking, leading to intellectual and moral error. And two of my chief life goals are being right and acting rightly.[4]

7. All else aside, getting angry is aversive for me. I don't "love to hate" anything or anyone. I wish to live in harmony with others, especially people I know personally.

As I rattle off these points in my head, I nervously visualize you getting angrier. So as usual, I'm not going to tell you what I'm really thinking. Still, after making full allowance for (2), here's a harsh truth: When you kill the messenger, your ignorance is culpable.[5] Your obliviousness to my concerns is a vice. Calm People like me deserve better.

Sincerely,

Calm Person

November 22, 2016

Notes

1. Caplan, Bryan. "My Life of Appeasement." *EconLog*, August 5, 2014.
2. Caplan, Bryan. "Escape from the Ivory Tower: Obscure Academic Economic Concepts Worth Knowing." *EconLog*, June 18, 2010.
3. Caplan, Bryan. "Why Most Economists Are Hawks and Why They Might Be Wrong." *EconLog*, April 27, 2005.
4. Caplan, Bryan. "Against Human Weakness." *EconLog*, September 2, 2009.
5. Caplan, Bryan. "Mao's Great Famine and Depraved Indifference." *EconLog*, February 12, 2011.

The Silent Suffering
of the Non-Neurotic

Negative emotions like sadness, anger, and fear tend to come as a package. Personality psychologists call this package "Neuroticism."[1] There's a spectrum, of course. At the high end of Neuroticism, we have people like *Seinfeld*'s George Costanza, who finds misery and outrage wherever he turns.[2] At the low end, we have people like *Seinfeld*'s Cosmo Kramer, who discovers amusement and excitement around every corner.[3]

Having a Neurotic personality is not fun, and Neurotics rarely let us forget it. This doesn't imply, however, that they're victims. By acting on their sadness, anger, and fear, Neurotics routinely make the people around them sadder, angrier, and more fearful. Parallel claims hold for non-Neurotics. They rarely complain, but that doesn't imply they're *not* victims.

How exactly does society victimize the non-Neurotic? Look at the news — or, in an election year, politics. It's a parade of stories crafted to make every onlooker feel sadness, anger, and fear. It's a pan-ideological problem: Left and right disagree on

142

many things, but both tribes of activists want you to get upset about something every day. Take a look at the stories your friends shared on Facebook today. How many *aren't* a thinly-veiled demand for negative affect?[4]

If your Neuroticism is high or even average, you probably aren't even aware that you're imposing on others. For you, calling on people to be sad, angry, or afraid is on par with asking them to walk with their eyes open. And since non-Neurotics aren't prone to complain, it's easy to remain oblivious to their concerns.

Actually, as a self-identified non-Neurotic, I should say, "*our* concerns." Though I loathe to complain, I can't stand to see my people suffer any longer. Sadness, anger, and fear do not come naturally to us. We don't "love to hate" things. And though we are happy to lend a sympathetic and constructive ear to your concrete problems, we don't want to be part of the vicissitudes of your abstract offense.

I know Neurotics are highly unlikely to change their personalities. But it would be nice if you showed us non-Neurotics a little consideration. And we so rarely ask for *anything*! Without reproach, I ask you this: Please, stop trying to make us feel what you feel.

Thanks in advance!

November 15, 2016

Notes

1. "Neuroticism." *Wikipedia.*
2. "George Constanza." *Wikipedia.*
3. "Cosmo Kramer." *Wikipedia.*
4. "Negative affectivity." *Wikipedia.*

A.B.A.: Always Be Advising

I often annoy other economists by giving advice. "Economists are supposed to describe behavior, not change it," they insist. But they couldn't be more wrong. Economics is inherently advisory. Anytime an economist notices a discrepancy between (a) the world as it is, and (b) the world as people believe it to be, economics *implies* advice.

Suppose an economist knows that the true price of driving a mile is $.25. If X falsely believes that the price is $.23 per mile, the economist has every right to tell him, "You drive too much."

"Too much" by what standard? By whatever standards X happens to hold.

On the other hand, if X falsely believes that the price is $.27 per mile, the economist has every right to tell him, "You drive too little."

"Too little" by what standard? By whatever standards X happens to hold.

The same applies if X under- or over-estimates the toxicity of cigarettes, the distance from Boston to New York, or the probability of getting tenure. If you over-estimate costs or under-estimate benefits, economics tells you to start doing more. If you under-estimate costs or over-estimate benefits, economics tells you to start doing less.

Notice the huge difference between economic advice and, say, medical advice.[1] The typical doctor will tell you, "Cigarettes are bad for your health, so stop smoking." For an economist to give smoking advice, in contrast, he needs to know more than the mere fact that smoking has a downside. He needs to discover a discrepancy between *actual* and *perceived* downsides. Do you under-estimate the health risks of smoking? Then economics tell you to smoke less. Do you over-estimate the health risks of smoking? Then economics tells you to smoke *more*. Unlike doctors, economists know how to give advice and respect pluralism at the same time.

Of course, a long list of caveats is implicit.[2] If you're making a discrete choice, you need to interpret "buy more" as "be more willing to buy" and "buy less" as "be less willing to buy." If you simply don't enjoy a product, you should interpret "buy more" as "buy the same or more." If some people over-estimate and others under-estimate, you need to give the two groups opposite advice. Etc. It's OK to quibble, but the logic of what Patri Friedman calls "directional rationality" is hard to escape.

Bottom line: Once you discover a discrepancy between the world as it is and the world as people perceive it to be, economic science and economic advice are perfectly compatible.[3] The only economists who should give no advice are the freakishly unperceptive souls who have failed to discover a single discrepancy between the world as it is and the world as people perceive it to be.

July 5, 2011

Notes

1. Caplan, Bryan. "Should I Take to Drink?" *EconLog*, April 1, 2006.
2. Caplan, Bryan. "Carroll, Wilkinson, and Four Demand Curves." *EconLog*, April 14, 2011.
3. Caplan, Bryan. "The Charge of Creepiness." *EconLog*, January 26, 2009.

The Charge of Creepiness

C K, an EconLog reader, writes:[1]

> I find your obsession with the topic of people's
> personal choices to be deeply creepy. Also, the
> fact that your starting point is that they are in
> error is a textbook example of bad logic, e.g.,
> assuming what you need to prove. Furthermore,
> it is highly against the logic of economics to as-
> sume that you know people's preferences and/
> or utility function better than they do (cf., con-
> sumer sovereignty).

I'm not sure how many other people find my "obsession"
creepy, but I doubt that CK is alone. My defense: I don't see
why it's any more creepy to give advice about family size than
advice about personal finance or home theater design. I'm not
trying to bully anyone, just share some relevant arguments
and evidence with the world. What's wrong with that?

Perhaps the complaint is that having a child is much more "personal" than picking a mutual fund or a high-definition projector. I agree with the premise — whether to have a child is especially personal. But that's no reason to spurn advice, as I explain in the preface to *Selfish Reasons to Have More Kids* (work in progress):

> Whether to have a child is obviously one of life's most personal decisions. Just because a decision is personal, however, does not mean that "Whatever decision you make is the right one for you." Precisely because the decision to have a child is complicated, its consequences are easy to misjudge. Your personal decision can be way off — and if you make up your mind too quickly, you're only cheating yourself.

Is it creepy to claim to know someone's preferences/utility function better than they do? A key point in my argument is that I don't need to claim any such thing. When an economist tells you to diversify your portfolio, he isn't trying to overrule your values; he's trying to explain the best way to achieve your values. The same thing goes with my advice about family size.

I've also noticed that some libertarians see my arguments as somehow unlibertarian. But I've never called for government to pressure people into having children; indeed, I favor many policy changes that I admit are anti-natalist (such as abolishing public schooling). The key point, though, is that *there's nothing unlibertarian about giving advice*.

So is there anything creepy about my project? I just don't see it. I'll admit there's such a thing as unwanted advice. Face-to-face, I rarely give advice unless someone asks for it.

But what could be less obtrusive than putting advice in writing on a blog, where the curious can read it, and the not-so-curious can scroll down to the next post?

January 26, 2009

Notes

1. Caplan, Bryan. "Why People Don't Want More Kids, and What It Means." *EconLog,* January 25, 2009.

Pax Libertaria

As a rule, I dislike shouting matches. But I especially dislike shouting matches between people I largely agree with. As a libertarian, this puts me in an uncomfortable position, because many libertarians seem to relish shouting matches — even, or especially, with other libertarians.

What is so bad about shouting matches?

First, they aren't persuasive to people who don't already agree with you. In other words, they aren't persuasive at all.[1]

Second, giving into anger makes it harder to tell truth from falsehood.

Third, as someone other than Buddha said, "Holding onto anger is like drinking poison and expecting the other person to die."[2] The main person who suffers when you're angry is you.

Fourth, assuming both sides share worthwhile goals, shouting matches have a clear deadweight cost. The time you spend

151

shouting at each other could have been spent cooperating to accomplish something good. (Or at least independently accomplishing distinct good things).

If my assessment is correct, why do people ever engage in shouting matches? While I can imagine someone defending shouting matches on their merits, the main excuse I hear is: "The other side started it."

One problem with this story is that both sides usually have some reason to point fingers. Take the recent debate on the shortage of libertarian women.[3] While I disagree with much of Thomas Woods' reply, this passage resonated with me:

> Julie's critics can't conclude their attack without unbosoming the lasting trauma of the whole episode for them: today, because of Julie's video, they're "a little embarrassed to admit" they're libertarians. Poor babies. To my knowledge, they have not expressed any embarrassment when libertarians have (for example) gratuitously insulted the religious beliefs of tens of millions of Americans in crude and ignorant ways. I suppose that's designed to bring people into the fold?[4]

The sensible lesson to draw, of course, would be that libertarians should stop gratuitously insulting anyone. But if you stick to, "Who *started* gratuitously insulting people?," Woods could easily be correct. (Indeed, in the past I have personally been guilty of gratuitously insulting common religious beliefs, for no good reason. I apologize). If you're really going to persist in a shouting match on the grounds that the other side started it, it's quite possible that detailed historical investigation will reveal that your side started it. Worse, much depends on how you define the "sides."

In any case, if shouting matches are as counter-productive as I claim, it makes little difference who first left the path of civility. It really does take two to tango. If you find yourself in a shouting match, search your *own* words and behavior to see if you have needlessly provoked your opponents. Perhaps an apology is in order. If you're ambivalent, the wise err on the side of contrition. If, after a healthy adjustment for self-serving bias, you find yourself above reproach, it still pays to turn the other cheek, to talk to your opponent as if he were your best friend. While you'll still probably fail to persuade, you drastically increase your prospects.

You might reply, "The point of the shouting match isn't to persuade the other side. It's to persuade spectators that I shouldn't be blamed for the other side's embarrassing words." Perhaps. But if spectators are that easily confused, it's probably more effective to get the other side to stop embarrassing you. If so, which sounds more effective to you?

"Stop *embarrassing* me, you horrible excuse for a libertarian!"

or

"Two of my opponents' seven complaints about me are fair, and I'm going to stop doing these two things."

Note that I say "more effective" not "fully effective" or even "highly effective." As far as I know, there are no highly effective methods of persuasion in these matters. But some remain better than others.

My claims about shouting matches are completely general. But of course I'm most eager to end shouting matches between people close to me. Accordingly I propose a Pax Libertaria — a Libertarian Peace. The terms of the peace: Individual libertarians *unilaterally* pledge to defuse shouting matches by (a) meticulously searching their own words and actions for short-comings, (b) erring strongly on the side of making amends for their arguable shortcomings, and (c) turning the other cheek when the other side shouts at them despite their blamelessness. This could mean ignoring the other side, or politely responding to their substantive arguments without further comment.

To avoid misunderstanding, the Pax Libertaria certainly doesn't follow from libertarian principles. People have every right to engage in shouting matches, no matter how destructive. But as libertarians often say, the fact that you have a right to do X does not mean that it is right for you to do X. The Pax Libertaria is a roadmap to peace *for* libertarians. It's an attempt to increase the effectiveness of libertarian persuasion by reducing the frequency of libertarian infighting. If the Pax Libertaria seems like it's asking a lot, I say you have nothing to lose but your anger. Give Pax a chance.

January 7, 2013

Notes

1. Caplan, Bryan. "Principles of Good Debating." *EconLog*, July 28, 2010.
2. "Holding onto anger is like..." *Fake Buddha*.
3. Caplan, Bryan. "Women, Liberty, Marketing, and Social Science." *EconLog*, January 4, 2013.
4. Woods, Tom. "The Central Committee Has Handed Down Its Denunciation." *Tom Woods*, January 4, 2013.

Conversion:
The Quantity/Quality Trade-off

onfession: Whenever I write, I'm looking for converts.
I don't just want to share some information. I want
to change how my readers think – and how they see
themselves.

When I read other proselytizing thinkers, however, I cringe.
I cringe not merely because I disagree with their conclusions.
And I certainly don't object to the conversion motive itself. I
cringe, rather, because my competitors seem far too focused
on the *quantity* of their converts rather than their *quality*.

How can I tell? If your main goal is to convince as many
people as possible, you naturally focus on emotional appeals —
especially to anger, fear, and disgust. Everyone feels these emotions, so everyone's a potential convert. If you bother making
arguments at all, build your case around vivid stories, not step-
by-step arguments. Don't bother trying to pass an Ideological
Turing Test for opposing views; you'll just confuse your audience.[1] In fact, don't bother anticipating and answering the best
objections to your views. Just troll and move on.[2] Why respond

to arguments most of your potential converts have never even heard?

In contrast, if your main goal is to *improve* the intellectual quality of people on "your side," you do the opposite. Start by urging your allies to calm down, because anger, fear, and disgust impede careful reasoning.[3] Then, review popular arguments for your allies' views — and point out flaws in said arguments. Finally, offer better arguments — and more reasonable conclusions. Along the way, you'll eagerly address the best objections you've encountered — and try to present them as skillfully as their best advocates. By the end, most of your potential audience will have wandered away in anger, fear, and disgust. But the few who remain will be better thinkers and better people.

I can't honestly claim to focus solely on quality. Frankly, it gets a little dull. But from where I'm standing, most public intellectuals focus *almost exclusively* on quantity. This is hardly surprising for slower-witted pundits; maybe they can't do any better. But when I see brilliant minds demagoguing, I'm aghast.[4] Even if they made converts by the boatload, I'd be ashamed to emulate them.

Admittedly, you could accuse me of sour grapes. My quantity-conversion skills are, at best, weak. My quality-conversion skills, in contrast, are pretty good. Give me an hour with someone who sympathizes with my general views, and I can reliably inculcate more reasonable versions of those views.

And if you give me ten minutes every day on EconLog, I can do much more. You will not be numerous, my readers. But you will be marvelous!

December 8, 2016

Notes

1. Caplan, Bryan. "The Ideological Turing Test." *EconLog*, June 20, 2011.
2. Caplan, Bryan. "Against Trolling." *EconLog*, April 20, 2016.
3. Caplan, Bryan. "The Mellow Heuristic." *EconLog*, April 24, 2015.
4. Caplan, Bryan. "Demagoguery Explained." *EconLog*, May 3, 2014.

Say It Loud, Say It Proud

If you were in marketing, would you take this advice?

1. To "raise the status of intelligence and analytical thinking," *don't...*

...stand for instrumental rationality, for Science, for attitudes which go beyond traditional religion, for the conquering of limits, for probabilistic reasoning, and for the notion that the subject sees hidden possibilities and resources which more traditional observers do not.[1]

Instead, give to mainstream charity.

2. If you value economics, keep it to yourself:[2]

If you are the economically informed member of your family, or perhaps even an economist, don't flaunt it. Hide its universal nature or widespread applicability. Do not present economic wisdom as a matter of principle or a general way of thinking about life.

3. If you're a libertarian, stop attacking the New Deal and jump on the scare-of-the-week bandwagon:[3]

> I would like to restructure classical liberalism, or libertarianism — whatever we call it — around these new and very serious threats to liberty. Let's not fight the last battle or the last war. Let's not obsess over all the interventions represented by the New Deal, even though I would agree that most of those policies were bad ideas.

The source of all three pieces of advice is my colleague Tyler Cowen. Notice the pattern? In each case, he urges people to whom he's officially sympathetic to abandon their main arguments *without argument*, and try to curry favor by doing and saying "normal" things.

Frankly, I can't imagine marketing experts recommending a Cowenian approach. Instead, they'd tell you the obvious: If you've got good ideas to sell, don't be shy. Affably explain why you're right and your critics are wrong.[4] Say it loud and say it proud. Once you reach market saturation, you might want to mix up your marketing a bit. But until you're a household name, clearly and boldly make your point. And remember — there's no point in pandering to those who will never buy your product, anyway.

July 10, 2010

Notes

1. Cowen, Tyler. "Why Pick On Cryonics." *Marginal Revolution*, July 10, 2010.
2. Caplan, Bryan. "Closet Your Inner Economist?" *EconLog*, June 25, 2007.
3. Cowen, Tyler. "The Paradox of Libertarianism." *Cato Unbound*, March 11, 2007.
4. Caplan, Bryan. "The Libertarian Case for Friendliness." *EconLog*, July 14, 2008.

Rand vs. Evolutionary Psychology: Part 1

I want you to observe, that those who cry the loudest about their disillusionment, about the failure of virtue, the futility of reason, the impotence of logic — are those who have a-chieved the full, exact, logical result of the ideas they preached, so mercilessly logical that they dare not identify it.

— Ayn Rand, *Atlas Shrugged*

The new Rand bio, Anne Heller's *Ayn Rand and the World She Made*, is almost hypnotic.[1] I read over two hundred pages yesterday, finished the book at 1 AM, and woke up two hours early thinking about it. While I already knew all the main facts and most of the details, Heller's a great storyteller, especially after the first two chapters.

The highlight is her account of the rise and fall of the New

York Objectivist movement.[2] It's a story of scary contrasts between theory and reality. The most striking: Rand and her closest followers were supposed to be amazingly happy because of their uniquely rational philosophy, but in practice they were openly angry and secretly miserable.

What went wrong? It is easy to account for some of the facts on strictly Randian lines. Nathaniel and Barbara Branden were Rand's closest followers. Nathaniel began an affair with Rand, and Barbara consented, even though Barbara hated the idea from the start and Nathaniel quickly lost interest in his aging mistress. In so doing, the Brandens betrayed their principles: They failed to stand up for their own interests, and wound up habitually lying to her. Rand's view of happiness ("Happiness is a state of non-contradictory joy — a joy without penalty or guilt, a joy that does not clash with any of your values and does not work for your own destruction") specifically predicts that the Brandens would be anguished as a result.[3]

So far, so good. But why would the Brandens feel the slightest temptation to deviate from Objectivist principles? And why was Rand herself so unhappy? Heller writes:

> Most of the time, she was adamant that her emotional condition was a natural response to intolerable circumstances.

However:

> She leaned more heavily on her heir [Nathaniel Branden] for aid in untangling her "premises," some of which she sometimes conceded must be wrong…

I have a simple explanation for *all* of these patterns: Objectivists defied the many truisms about human nature that evolutionary psychology later came to explain.[4] Truisms like:

1. Good looks and youth are *very* important for sexual attraction — especially from a male point of view.
2. People feel jealous when their mates have sex with other people.
3. Lying is often a convenient way to avoid your mate's jealousy.

On the Randian view, "a man's sexual choice is the result and the sum of his fundamental convictions."[5] So why wouldn't her affair with Nathaniel be a great success? Their shared "fundamental convictions" should cause enduring love — never mind the 25-year age difference! Barbara has no reason to resent sharing her husband; in fact, she should be flattered that the great Rand so admires him. And of course, if Nathaniel wanted to end the affair, he would have no motive to lie, because Rand would not be jealous of any woman fit to replace her.

Unfortunately for Rand, her theory smashes against billions of years of evolution. Yes, mutual admiration and shared values have *something* to do with sexual attraction. But humans with Rand-approved emotions would have been at a *massive* reproductive disadvantage. Men don't get descendants by pursuing fifty-year-old women, no matter how brilliant they are. Jealousy also serves a vital evolutionary function: It protects men from cuckoldry, and women from sharing or losing the support of the father of her children.

Trying to argue people out of these extremely *adaptive* feelings — or pretend they don't exist — is absurd. Heller shows that even Rand wasn't able to completely ignore common sense. She brought up the age difference before she started the affair, and occasionally wondered whether it bothered Nathaniel. But when he said it didn't matter, she took his word for it. Surely her greatest disciple wouldn't lie merely to avoid her jealous wrath?

So how exactly does evolutionary psychology explain the misery, the jealousy, the lying? When Rand and her followers tried to wish away obvious facts about humans' emotional constitution, their feelings didn't change. But they made each other miserable *pretending* that they felt the way they were *supposed* to feel. Rand and Nathaniel had to pretend that Nathaniel was attracted to Rand. Their spouses had to pretend that they weren't jealous. Rand and Nathaniel had to pretend that they believed that their spouses weren't jealous. The more they tried to talk themselves into having feelings contrary to human nature, the worse they felt. Nathaniel coped not by admitting error, but by finding a mistress and lying to cover it up. Since Rand had already ruled out the obvious explanation for Nathaniel's behavior, she went on a wild goose chase to find the "real" explanation. Etc.

Sigh. As Rand says, "[F]acts cannot be altered by a wish, but they can destroy the wisher." I give her a lot of credit for emphasizing that human beings are potentially rational animals. But she evaded (yes, evaded!) the fact that human beings are *invariably* animals — and paid the price.[6]

January 12, 2020

Notes

1. Heller, Anne. *Ayn Rand and the World She Made*, 2009.
2. "Objectivist Movement." *Wikipedia*.
3. "Happiness." *Ayn Rand Lexicon*.
4. "Evolutionary Psychology." *Wikipedia*.
5. "The Meaning of Sex." *Ayn Rand Institute*.
6. "Evasion." *Ayn Rand Lexicon*.

Rand vs. Evolutionary Psychology:
Part 2

I want you to observe, that those who cry the loudest about their disillusionment, about the failure of virtue, the futility of reason, the impotence of logic — are those who who have a-chieved the full, exact, logical result of the ideas they preached, so mercilessly logical that they dare not identify it.

— Ayn Rand, *Atlas Shrugged*

Ayn Rand praised the virtues of individualism and in-dependence to the skies. In *Atlas Shrugged*, philoso-pher Hugh Akston tells Dagny, "Consider the reasons which make us certain that we are right... but not the fact that we are certain. If you are not convinced, ignore our certainty. Don't be tempted to substitute our judgment for your own." Her heroes do whatever they think is right, regardless of what anyone thinks. It's quite a vision.

In the late 1950s, Rand's writings inspired a full-blown Objectivist counter-culture centered around New York City. And what did this counter-culture look like? Anne Heller's excellent *Ayn Rand and the World She Made* paints a frightening picture.[1] The counter-culture didn't just fall short of the Randian virtues. It radically contradicted them:

> During Saturday-night socials with members of the Collective [Rand's inner circle of followers] and their spouses, friends and younger guests, "enormous enthusiasm was expected for her every deed and utterance," Branden told an audience in 1996.[2] She discouraged the kind of probing or "invalid" questions that she had been happy to answer in the 1950s... Rand increasingly judged her votaries' merit on the basis of their "sense of life," or subconscious attitude toward the grandeur and perfectability of man, and encouraged them to do the same with one another... The new emphasis on "sense of life" placed devotees' longings, fears, tastes, sexual impulses — anything — on the table for approval or condemnation. "Most people were walking on eggshells," recalled Henry Holzer, who joined the inner circle as Rand's "intellectual bodyguard"...

Just a few examples:

> A slip of the tongue by an Objectivist who liked Alfred Hitchcock's *Psycho* or who secretly didn't like the paintings of... Spanish surrealist Jose Manuel

167

Capuletti, could bring accusations of mysticism, whim worship, malevolence, or an attitude of "anti-life." If a transgression suggested disloyalty or simply that someone was "not my kind of person," often no amount of prior goodwill made any difference. "She was the Evel Knievel of leaping to conclusions," said Hessen, who himself went through a number of painful episodes.[3] Although she typically forgave isolated lapses, tantrums and purges became more common in the late 1960s.

While Heller quotes Nathaniel Branden, her sources reveal that he was probably worse than Rand herself:

It was typically Branden who took charge of the denunciation of followers who had strayed, and sometimes he revealed information from his therapy sessions with them. "There was very little psychological privacy in those days," he offered as an explanation to an interviewer in 1999. "Everything that was wrong with anybody or was thought to be wrong was publicly discussed..." By the early 1960s, he "was constantly denouncing," Barbara recalled, and because he was "everybody's therapist, his denunciation was much more damaging than Ayn's."[4]

I attended the "official" Objectivist summer seminar back in 1989 — the year of the David Kelley purge — and everything that Heller writes fits my experience.[5]

OK, so Ayn Rand created a cult. What does this have to do

with evolutionary psychology? Simple: Contrary to Rand, the fact that human beings care about the opinions of the people around them doesn't stem from philosophical error. It stems from evolution. Human beings evolved in small groups where good relations were vital for survival. People who weren't interested in other people's opinions had trouble staying alive and reproducing. Caring about the opinions of others isn't as immutable as our sexual preferences, but it's very deeply rooted.[6] Consider: How much would I have to pay you to walk in front of an audience of a hundred strangers and make a fool of yourself?

Rand was no exception. She thought that her affair with Branden was morally above reproach, but made every effort to keep it secret. Why? Because unlike John Galt, she shared our normal human concern about the opinions of other people — including complete strangers:

> [A]nother thought struck her and put her in a panic. If he had been underhanded enough to deceive her about his feelings toward her for months or years on end, what else might he be capable of? Would he do something terrible to embarrass her in public or discredit her ideas...? "I can't predict what he'll do, and I'm terrified of what may happen to my name and reputation!" she cried in despair. Growing tired and tearful as the night wore on, she murmured, "My life is over. He took away this earth."

If people really could stop caring about other people's o-pinions, Rand's counter-culture never would have gotten off the ground. Within five minutes, prospective members would have adamantly disagreed with Rand about something or other, and she would have purged them. Her counter-culture took root precisely because even avowed individualists will feign agreement in order to fit in.

Ironically, individualist doctrine made the Randian counter-culture *especially* totalitarian. Most normal movements explicitly accept appeals to authority, consensus, civility, etc. So while they're bossy, they don't ask their members to live a lie. Catholics can freely admit that the Pope is in charge. What the Pope says, goes! Objectivists, in contrast, couldn't just honestly submit to Rand's authority. They had to pretend to accept all of Rand's positions *on their merits.*

If Rand really wanted to build an individualist sub-culture, she would have done so in an evolutionarily informed way. If people naturally care about the opinions of others, jumping on people is a good way to get dishonest conformity, but a bad way to get an honest exchange of ideas. Instead, an individualist sub-culture must be built upon *tolerance and honesty.* I'd suggest three key norms:

1. Don't think less of people who sincerely disagree.
2. Do think less of people who insincerely agree.
3. Do think less of people who think less of people who sincerely disagree.

I don't claim that these norms are *easy*. It's tough for humans to follow them perfectly. But they're do-able — and given human nature, they're self-reinforcing. In fact, these guidelines are pillars of the legendary GMU lunch. Our tradition is now in its thirteenth year, and I'm proud to say that unlike the Objectivists, we've never purged a member.

January 29, 2010

Notes

1. Heller, Anne. *Ayn Rand and the World She Made*, 2009.
2. "Nathaniel Branden." *Wikipdia*.
3. "Robert Hessen." *Wikipedia*.
4. "Barbara Branden." *Wikipedia*.
5. Kelly, Michael. "Selective Timeline and Links of the Kelly-Peikoff Schism." *Objectivist Living*, August 19, 2006.
6. Caplan, Bryan. "Rand vs. Evolutionary Pscyhology: Part 1." *EconLog*, January 12, 2010.

The Futility of Quarreling When There Is No Surplus to Divide

I magine two people have the following relationship options:

Option A: Date
Option B: Be Friends
Option C: Stop Seeing Each Other

Person #1's preference ordering is: {A, C, B}. In English, #1 most prefers to date, and least prefers to just be friends.

Person #2's preference ordering is: {B, C, A}. In English, #2 most prefers to just be friends, and least prefers to date.

In popular stereotypes, Person #1 is male, and Person #2 is female. But role reversal is probably common, too.

Given these preferences, anything other than C naturally leads to bad feelings. Person #1 resents being stuck in "the friend zone." Person #2 resents Person #1's view that being friends is an imposition or probationary situation. It's easy to see how they might angrily quarrel with each other, with Person #1 harping on his superiority to whoever Person #2

172

dates, and Person #2 pointing out that Person #1 should be grateful for their friendship. The fight could get really ugly, as in the web comic "The Friend-Zoner vs. Nice Guy."[1]

On reflection, though, this quarreling is the epitome of futility. Sure, argument has been known to change preferences. But *these* preferences? Is #1 really going to argue #2 into feeling attracted to him when she's not? Is #2 really going to argue #1 out of his feelings of yearning and rejection? Extremely unlikely. Quarreling is ultimately a form of bargaining. With preference orderings {A, C, B} and {B, C, A}, the only mutually beneficial bargain is ceasing to deal with each other. And since either person can instantly and unilaterally jump to C by saying, "So long, have a nice life," what's the point of quarreling to get there?

If you're deeply economistic, you'll naturally ask, "Why not consider Option D: side payments?" "If you agree to just be friends, I'll do your laundry" or "If you agree to date, I'll pay for every meal." But in many cases — if not most — offering or accepting side payments feels so degrading that neither side can accept it. Option D is off the table because the parties' expanded rankings are {A, C, B, D} and {B, C, A, D}.

Needless to say, people have imperfect information about other people's preferences. Indeed, people have imperfect information about their *own* preferences. Yet in many real world relationships, preferences are fairly obvious — and my analysis applies.

I suspect that many non-economists will dismiss this whole approach as "overly analytical." I beg to differ. Widespread futile quarreling is a strong sign that emotional approaches have failed. The only way out is to calm down and admit that bad matches aren't anyone's fault. When two people want incompatible things, they should politely say goodbye and move on with their lives. Almost everyone can see this by the time they're 40.[2] With economics by your side, you can attain this enlightened state at once.

February 11, 2014

Notes

1. "The Friend-Zoner vs. Nice Guy." *Quora.*
2. Caplan, Bryan. "40 Things I Learned in My First 40 Years." *EconLog,* April 8, 2011.

Malevolence and Misunderstanding

Lancelot: Your rage has unbalanced you. You, sir, would fight to the death, against a knight who is not your enemy. Over a stretch of road you could easily ride around.

Arthur: So be it. To the death!

— Excalibur

Question #1: How many times in your life have you lost a friend because one of you malevolently decided to hurt to the other?

Question #2: How many times in your life have you lost a friend over a misunderstanding?

I am glad to report that I have lost few friends in my life. But as far as I can tell, all of the rare exceptions were driven by misunderstandings. Someone spoke rashly, which hurt someone's feelings, which led to retaliation, which led to more hurt feelings, and so on. Or, someone acted as they thought proper, but someone else perceived otherwise, which led to offense, which led to counter-offense. The same goes for all the people I know well. They've lost many friends, but years later they flounder to explain the *casus belli*.[1]

Is my corner of the world unusually free of sheer evil? Probably. Still, I doubt my experience is unusual. I bet that most readers have lost at least *five times* as many friends to misunderstandings as they have to malevolence.

How can you tell the difference between malevolence and misunderstanding? Try this helpful thought experiment. Imagine both sides *calmly* describe what they saw with their own eyes and heard with their own ears to a *neutral outsider*. If the outsider would tell both sides to forget the dispute and stay friends, you had a misunderstanding. If the outsider would say, "This is a bad match," you *still* had a misunderstanding; just one that's likely to recur. But if the outsider would tell one of you, "Get away from this toxic person," you saw — or were — malevolence.*

Why appeal to "neutral outsiders"? Well, the main reason misunderstandings arise is because most human beings rush to assume malevolence. Indeed, this is built into the very concept of the "misunderstanding"! Sure, *I* sometimes speak rashly. Sure, *I'm* no mind reader. When my friends speak rashly to me, or fail to understand my feelings, however, the default explanation is not that they spoke hastily or failed to see the world from my perspective. The default explanation is that they consciously decided to make me suffer.

Yes, it's childish to think this way. But what can I say? People are childish.

Small example: Friday I was shopping with my sons. My back was hurting, so they were pushing the cart. When I got in line, a woman immediately pulled up her cart behind me. By this point, my sons were ten feet away. When I asked her to make room for our cart, she grew angry: "Well that's *strange!*" Even my highly visible back brace was not enough to make her wonder about my situation. When I meekly got out of the way and offered to let her go ahead of me, she huffed and moved to the next lane. To me, this was a textbook example of a misunderstanding. Still, I suspect she went home and told her family about how awful I was. I made the effort to understand where she was coming from, but somehow she gazed into the heart of a total stranger and saw malevolence.

You could object, "Yours is hardly an original point. Parents and teachers routinely alert children to the risk of misunder-standings." Fair enough. My claim, however, is that this lesson rarely sinks in. Adults remain prone to misinterpret mere mis-understandings as malevolence. Indeed, there are mighty social and political movements that angrily strive to amplify this error — to ascribe malevolence recklessly, and demean those who ask us to mimic the perspective of a neutral outsider when conflict arises.

These days, the Me Too movement is the highest-profile example. When you carefully listen to the public accusations, their severity varies tremendously. The case of Bill Cosby is light-years from the cases of Louie C.K. or Aziz Ansari.[2] Is it possible that the latter two celebrities were involved in mis-understandings that bizarrely became national crises? Entirely possible. But most Me Too activists don't just gloss over this possibility; they view those who muse, "Maybe it's all a big mis-understanding" with hostility. At the risk of creating a new misunderstanding, my reaction to most Me Too scandals is precisely, "Maybe it's all a big misunderstanding." Indeed, I maintain that we should presume that conflicts are mis-understandings in the absence of strong evidence to the contrary.

How far should we apply this insight? Far indeed. Even

tiny slights, uncharitably interpreted, often spiral out of control.[3] So let us assess behavior with perspective and charity. Much conflict between Democrats and Republicans rests on misunderstandings.[4] Much of the conflict between Black Lives Matter and Blue Lives Matter conflict rests on misunderstandings. So does much of the Israeli-Palestinian conflict.[5] Indeed, part of the reason why I'm a pacifist is that so many international conflicts are plainly rooted in misunderstandings.[6] (If you can't wait to scoff, "So the Nazis just had a big misunderstanding with the rest of Europe?," you are fostering a misunderstanding between us. Over a stretch of road you could easily ride around).

If we fully accepted the prevalence of misunderstandings, couldn't a malevolent person take advantage of us? I'm afraid so. Fortunately, that's a minor danger compared to the opposite mistake. Remember: When you lose a friend over a misunderstanding, you don't merely mistreat a friend. You deprive yourself of friendship in a lonely world.

* A worse, but still tolerably good rule of thumb: If your own complaints against your former friend seem less compelling to you years later, you probably had a misunderstanding. If your complaints actually seem *more* compelling years later, malevolence is more plausible.

September 17, 2019

Notes

1. "Casus Belli." *Wikipedia*.
2. "Bill Cosby Sexual Assault Cases." *Wikipedia*. "Louis C. K." *Wikipedia*. North, Anna. "Aziz Ansari has Addressed His Sexual Assault Allegation. But He Hasn't Publicly Apologized." *Vox*, June 12, 2019.
3. Caplan, Bryan. "Escape from the Ivory Tower: Obscure Academic Economic Concepts Worth Knowing." *EconLog*, June 18, 2010.
4. Bacon, Perry. "Democrats are Wrong About Republicans. Republicans are Wrong About Democrats." *FiveThirtyEight*, June 26, 2018.
5. Caplan, Bryan. "The Economics of the Israeli-Palestinian Conflict." *EconLog*, February 8, 2005.
6. Caplan, Bryan. "Pacifism Redux." *EconLog*, July 13, 2011. Caplan, Bryan. "Why Most Economists are Hawks and Why They Might Be Wrong." *EconLog*, April 27, 2005.

How Can Guys Be
So Lazy Around the House?

The *Economist* blog shares one of its "favourite strategies for ramping down the gender war":[1]

> Men don't need to do more housework and childcare to achieve equality. Women just need to do less. My dad used to change the oil in our family cars. I certainly don't. I suffer exactly zero shame from the fact that I don't even know how. There are specialists who do this sort of thing. Real women's liberation and gender equality will come when social expectations shift enough to allow families to guiltlessly take full advantage of the returns to specialisation.

But why did a gender war arise in the first place? In my view, it is largely a case of misplaced resentment. When women see how little housework men do, they interpret it as "shirking" – a willful violation of basic norms of decency. Men, in turn, feel unfairly maligned by the accusation (or, perhaps more often, by the stink eye).[2]

Who is right? Let me just throw away any future career in couples counseling, and say: Usually, men.

The evidence: Look at the typical bachelor's apartment. Even when a man pays the full cost of cleanliness and receives the full benefit, he doesn't do much. Why not? Because the typical man doesn't care very much about cleanliness. When the bachelor gets married, he almost certainly starts doing *more* housework than he did when he was single. How can you call that shirking?

I would take the woman's side if the guy actually agreed to a-dopt her standards. But few marriage contracts are so explicit. All that well-meaning spouses can usually do is adhere to vague norms of decency, such as the Golden Rule. The problem with applying the Golden Rule to housework is that most men already give their wives at least as much help as they would like to receive themselves.

Declaring the typical man to be innocent of the accusations against him may not seem very helpful. But it is. If you think that someone is willfully shirking, you probably won't bother to bargain for better behavior. The shirker has already broken his word once; why should you believe he'll change? In contrast, if you can accept that a person is living up to his obligations as he understands them, it's a lot easier to amicably renegotiate. Furthermore, as some fascinating research shows, the hardest problems to cope with are those you blame on *other people*.[3] The false belief that your spouse is taking advantage of you isn't just bad for your marriage; it's bad for you.

January 23, 2008

Notes

1. "The Age of Hedonic Marriage." *The Economist*, January 18, 2008.
2. "Stink-Eye." *Urban Dictionary.*
3. Caplan, Bryan. "Happiness Research: Get Used to It." *EconLog*, March 1, 2006.

Dear Prudence

W ould a society made up of totally selfish human beings be worse than the society we have today? Could it even function? In last week's Inaugural James M. Buchanan Lecture, Deirdre McCloskey seemed to think that the obvious answers were Yes to the first question, and No to the second.[1] A society that practiced no virtue other than Prudence would be a disaster.

I'm not so sure.

Here's the key point: Suppose you were totally selfish. What are you currently doing that isn't *already* in your narrow self-interest? Not stealing? You'd be risking years in jail for stuff that you could safely buy with a little work. Not lying? Hmm, ever hear of the Boy Who Cried Wolf? Not giving to charity? How much do you give as it is? Refuse to help a friend in need? Before you say "It's not my problem," you'd be well-advised to google the phrase Tit-for-Tat.[2]

Frankly, your current behavior is probably very close to what Prudence alone recommends. Your subjective motivation may not be selfish, but you roughly "act as if" you were. And if we think in terms of the *selfish gene* rather than the selfish individual, apparent counter-examples like parenting fall naturally into place.[3]

Now suppose we repeat this exercise for everyone alive: Holding constant other people's behavior, how would you change your behavior if you were totally selfish? If each person answers "I wouldn't," then the status quo and Absolute Prudence are compatible.

Of course, this is an over-simplification. There would be some differences. But it's hard to say whether the reign of Prudence would make the world a better or worse place to live. Yes, charity to strangers would probably vanish, but selfless charity is already a pittance. (And Robin Hanson points out that even the selfish rich might give to charity to signal their wealth!) Drivers would be less courteous, and strangers ruder to one another.

But on the other hand, a world of pure Prudence has obvious advantages. Imagine a world where NO ONE was willing to die for a cause — country, religion, ethnicity, whatever. To make soldiers risk death, they'd have to start awfully poor and be richly rewarded. That sounds like a recipe for world peace to me. Similarly, imagine a world where NO ONE would try to hurt another person out of envy or spite. A great many conflicts would vanish, for, as Inigo Montoya says in the *Princess Bride*, "There's not a lot of money in revenge."[4]

Bottom line: A world of pure Prudence would be rough around the edges. But there's no reason to think it wouldn't work, and a lot of reason to think that it would be both safer and saner that the world we see today. "All you need is Love"? It would be prettier, but it's never going to happen. "All you need is Prudence," is the more realistic slogan for a better world, because it encourages people to do what they're in-clined to do anyway.

April 12, 2006

Notes

1. McCloskey, Deirdre. "The Hobbes Problem: From Machiavelli to Buchanan.": *Prudentia*.
2. "Tit for tat." *Oxford Dictionary*.
3. "The Selfish Gene." *Wikipedia*.
4. "The Princess Bride." *IMDB*.

The Bayesian Prisoners' Dilemma

S uppose someone sends you a new article claiming X. Intuitively, we think, "This will either make you more likely to believe X, or have no effect." Once you understand Bayesian reasoning, however, this makes no sense.[1] When someone sends you an article claiming X, you should ask yourself, *"Is this evidence stronger or weaker than I would have expected?"* If the answer is "stronger," then you should become more likely to believe X. However, if the answer is "weaker," then you should become *less* likely to believe X.

Thus, suppose you initially consider X absurd. When someone sends you some evidence in favor of X, you should update in favor of X if the evidence is less awful than expected. You should update against X, in contrast, only if the evidence is *even more awful* than expected.

Similarly, suppose you initially consider X absurd, but your brilliant friend nevertheless defends it. The fact that a brilliant person believes X is evidence in its favor. *Given* his brilliance, however, his arguments should only persuade you if they are *even better than you would have expected from one so brilliant.*

When a great mind offers mediocre arguments, you shouldn't merely be unmoved; you should be actively repelled: "That's the best you can do?!"

Example: One of the smartest people I know routinely sends me pro-"social justice" links on Twitter. As a result, I think even less of the movement than I previously did.[2] If even he fails to defend his view effectively, the view is probably truly devoid of merit.

What, however, should I conclude if this mighty intellect simply stopped sending me links? One possibility, of course, is that he's given up on me. Another possibility, though, is that he's exhausted his supply of evidence. At this point, he's got nothing better than... nothing.

The strange upshot: While Bayesian reasoning seems to imply that persuasive efforts are, on average, ineffective, there is a reason to keep arguing. Namely: Failure to argue is, on average, an admission of intellectual defeat. And by basic Bayesian principles, this in turn implies that the continuation of argument is at least weak evidence in favor of whatever you're arguing.

Stepping back, you can see a somewhat depressing conclusion. When people are perfect Bayesians, argument is a kind of Prisoners' Dilemma.[3]

If your opponent keeps arguing, you want to keep arguing so it doesn't look like you've run out of arguments.

If your opponent stops arguing, you want to keep arguing to emphasize that your opponent has run out of arguments.

As a result, both sides have an incentive to argue interminably. Which, as you may have noticed, they usually do.

Is there any ejector seat out of this intellectual trap? Yes. You could build a credible reputation for talking only when you have something novel to add to the conversation. Then instead of interpreting your silence as, "I've got nothing," Bayesian listeners will interpret it as, "I've rested my case."

[silence]

July 29, 2019

Notes

1. Yudkowsky, Eliezer. "An Intuitive Explanation of Bayes' Theorem." *Yudkowsky.*
2. Caplan, Bryan. "Good Manners vs. Political Correctness." *EconLog*, March 23, 2017.
3. Dixit, Avinash. "Prisoners' Dilemma." *EconLib Concise Encyclopedia of Economics.*

Do Labels and Good-versus-Evil Stories Drain IQ?

I'm a libertarian, a natalist, an atheist, a credentialist, an economist, an optimist, a behavioral economist, an elitist, a public choicer, a dualist, a Szaszian, a moral realist, an anti-communist, a pacifist, a hereditarian, a Masonomist, a moral intuitionist, a free-market Keynesian, a deontologist, a modal realist, a Huemerian, a Darwinian, the other kind of libertarian (=a believer in free will), and much more.[1] I could spend hours adding additional labels to the list. So it naturally caught my attention when Will Wilkinson remarked:[2]

> People call me libertarian but I don't in part because I'm not one, but mostly because I suspect that accepting any such label dings my IQ about 15 points.

If the IQ ding is additive, my many labels have long since reduced me to the intelligence of a cranberry. And even if the ding isn't additive, I don't have 15 IQ points to spare. Especially not if Tyler is right about the effect of good-versus-evil stories on IQ:

> As a simple rule of thumb, just imagine every time you're telling a good vs. evil story, you're basically lowering your IQ by ten points or more. If you just adopt that as a kind of inner mental habit, it's, in my view, one way to get a lot smarter pretty quickly. You don't have to read any books. Just imagine yourself pressing a button every time you tell the good vs. evil story, and by pressing that button you're lowering your IQ by ten points or more.[3]

I'm not as big on good-versus-evil stories as I am on self-labeling. I strive to be friendly to everyone.[4] I see noble adversaries, embarrassing allies, and various shades of grey. But there's a good-versus-evil story just below my surface, pitting reasonable, constructive, iconoclastic people who agree with me against the benighted masses and their emotional, whiny, conventional intellectual apologists. If Tyler and Will are both right, I'm down a minimum of 25 IQ points.

But what reason is there to believe that either Will or Tyler is correct? There are obviously *many* labels and *many* good-versus-evil stories that drain your effective IQ. Think Leninist, creationist, or astrologer. But it is equally obvious that many labels and many good-versus-evil stories *boost* your effective IQ. Think behavioral economist, Darwinian, or astronomer. ("And yet it moves.") Will and Tyler act as if these differences don't exist.[5]

Will and Tyler might protest that the *average* effect of labels and good-versus-evil stories is to reduce effective IQ. But they'd be wrong to do so. Agnostic, neutral thinkers have little to say and less to teach. Yes, it's better to suspend judgment rather than embrace error. But intellectual progress only occurs after someone discovers and publicizes good reasons to adopt an ism.

Aren't there intellectual risks of accepting labels and good-versus-evil stories? Sure. Labels can blind us to counter-evidence. Good-versus-evil stories give us an excuse to damn the messenger instead of considering his message. But the wise response is to strive to compensate for these specific risks – not to salute the intellectual equivalent of the Swiss flag. Indeed, when you really think about it, labels and good-versus-evil stories are unavoidable. Will's implicit label is "label-avoidism." Tyler's implicit good-versus-evil story is "the never-ending war between the good people who don't believe in good-versus-evil stories and the evil people who do."

Why am I so inclined to defend labels and good-versus-evil stories? Because when I review my life's work, I realize that I owe my life's work to my labels and stories.[6] You don't have to be a libertarian to appreciate *The Myth of the Rational Voter*, but without my libertarian goggles I would never have conceived the project.[7] The same goes for virtually everything I've written. You might point to something like "Why I Am Not an Austrian Economist" as a counter-example, but you should not.[8] I couldn't have written that piece if I weren't a lapsed Austrian, and wouldn't have written it if I didn't have a superior alternative (and label) to offer.

Labels and good-versus-evil often effectively drain IQ. Many drain 25 points or more. But there's no substitute for actually examining the specific content of the labels and stories. Stupid worldviews reduce IQ. Smart worldviews raise IQ. Declaring "a plague on all your houses" solves nothing.

April 9, 2012

Notes

1. Caplan, Bryan. "The Caplan-Hanson Debate: Liberty Versus Efficiency." *Bet On It*, March 5, 2024. Caplan, Bryan. "Population, Fertility, and Liberty." *Cato Unbound*. Caplan, Bryan. "Intellectual Autobiography of Bryan Caplan." *Bet On It*, September 12, 2023. Caplan, Bryan. "The Magic of Education." *EconLog*, November 28, 2011. Caplan, Bryan. "The Cynical Optimist." *EconLog*, September 17, 2005. Caplan, Bryan. "Solving the Mind-Body Problem: Dualism vs. Searle." *George Mason University*. Caplan, Bryan. "The Economics of Szasz: Preferences, Constraints, and Mental Illness." *Rationality and Society*, 2006. "Museum of Communism." *George Mason University*. Caplan, Bryan. "The Common Sense Case for Pacifism." *EconLog*, April 5, 2010. Caplan, Bryan. "The Tiger Mother versus Cost-Benefit Analysis." *EconLog*, February 2, 2011. Caplan, Bryan. "A Short Essay on the Freedom of Will." *George Mason University*.
2. Wilkinson, Will. "Politics vs. Empathy." *Big Think*, April 4, 2012.
3. Cowen, Tyler. "They Have Transcribed my TEDx Talk on Stories." *Marginal Revolution*, December 22, 2011.
4. Caplan, Bryan. "The Case for Libertarian Friendliness." *EconLog*, July 14, 2008.
5. "And yet it moves." *Wikipedia*.
6. "Curriculum Vitae." *bcaplan.com*.

7. Caplan, Bryan. *The Myth of the Rational Voter*, 2007.
8. Caplan, Bryan. "Why I Am Not an Austrian Economist." *George Mason University*.

I Was a Teenage Misanthrope

When I was a teenager, I viewed all of the following with antipathy: students not in honors classes, heavy metal fans, people who disliked classical music, stoners, athletes, cheerleaders, all but two of my teachers, car collectors, sports fans, smokers, drinkers, adults who hadn't gone to college, religious believers (especially Christians), liberals, conservatives, moderates, people bored by philosophy, anyone who didn't play Dungeons & Dragons, people who played Dungeons & Dragons without staying in character, Dungeon Masters for Monty Hall campaigns, people who didn't like classic literature, anyone who planned to major in math or science, people with low savings rates, people who were too cheap, gays, guys with girlfriends, punkers, proto-Goths, people who worked with their hands, fans of *Cheech and Chong*, people with low IQs, and girls who dated *anyone* on the preceding list.[1]

I was, in short, a teenage misanthrope.

Why was I such a misanthrope? If you asked me at the time, I probably would have said, "Because almost everyone is terrible." If you asked me, "Well, *why* is it so terrible to be any of these things?," I guess I would have simply added "People who challenge my misanthropy" to my list of antipathy.

Fortunately, virtually all of my misanthropy has melted away with age. I can honestly say that, on a typical day, absolutely *no one* upsets me. This is partly because I've constructed a Beautiful Bubble for myself.[2] The main reason, though, is that I've learned the wisdom of tolerance. Yes, most people are very different from me. Yes, I have little in common with most people. But why should I expect anything else? How other people live their lives is their business, not mine.

If I could go back in time, what would I tell my misanthropic teenage self? Roughly the following:

1. In many cases, you're just being silly. Say: "Oh, it's so *horrible* for someone to play Dungeons & Dragons incorrectly" or "Oh, it's so *awful* to dislike opera," without laughing. Can't do it, can you?

2. In many cases, people can't help being the way they are. People don't choose to have low IQ. So understanding rather than contempt is in order.

3. What about serious character flaws that people *can* help? For the most part, people are the main victims of their own character flaws. So just leave them alone and perhaps they'll learn.

4. *You* have a serious character flaw that you can help: misanthropy. And per #3, you're the main victim of your own flaw. Most people are totally unaware of your antipathy, even though your antipathy makes you unhappy every day. Put down your load of resentment and you'll feel a lot better.

5. Once you fix your misanthropy, you can focus on improving your life. Be constructive all day, every day. Focus on *how*

to avoid unpleasant experiences, not *who* to condemn. Take all the time you spend ruminating on everything you don't like, and spend it doing something you do like.

6. If you really think that only 1% of people are worth talking to, *search* for the 1% instead of lamenting their scarcity. If you're pleasant to everyone, you'll have a much larger pool of potential friends to choose from. Then you can enjoy life instead of complaining about it.

Would my teenage self have found my current self persuasive? Yes, actually. I learn slowly from experience, but quickly from explicit argument. Given twenty hours of conversation with a wiser version of myself, I would have abandoned misanthropy years ahead of schedule.

Oh well, better late than never.

May 1, 2013

Notes

1. "The Monty Haul Campaign." *Frontiernet.*
2. "Cheech and Chong." *Wikipedia.*
3. Caplan, Bryan. "My Beautiful Bubble." *EconLog,* March 19, 2012.

Made in the USA
Middletown, DE
06 September 2024